Here Be Wonders

July 15, 2024

To Dear Louise Gary too. and remembering Gary too. In solidarity with you both who also love Christ's church. No doubt Gary now sees The church more fully than we do! "Open your hand, this is for you."

Love & Prayers.
Nancy

Here Be Wonders

—— The Gospel's Pulse in Unsettled Times ——

Nancy Vernon Kelly

RESOURCE *Publications* · Eugene, Oregon

HERE BE WONDERS
The Gospel's Pulse in Unsettled Times

Resource Publications
An Imprint of Wipf and Stock Publishers
199 W. 8th Ave., Suite 3
Eugene, OR 97401

www.wipfandstock.com

PAPERBACK ISBN: 979-8-3852-1259-0
HARDCOVER ISBN: 979-8-3852-1260-6
EBOOK ISBN: 979-8-3852-1261-3

VERSION NUMBER 06/10/24

Dedicated to the people of First English Lutheran Church,[1]

St. Mark's Lutheran Church,

and the land on which they were planted and took root

—

Kitchener, Ontario Canada

1914–2018

1. First English Lutheran Church was the first English-speaking Lutheran faith community in Kitchener (formerly Berlin), Ontario. At the time, all the other Lutheran churches in town spoke German. When the congregation decided to build a new, bigger church, they chose a new name, St. Mark's, and a new site, the corner of King and Green Streets in the heart of the twin cities Kitchener and Waterloo.

Land Acknowledgement

A t an intersection in an area now known as downtown Kitchener, there once was a church. I wandered into that church as a newcomer to Canada, a newcomer to Christ and was welcomed with open arms, plates of food, hugs, support and love. The stories you will read in this book, stories of happenings at this intersection, describe this welcome, the welcome of love.

This intersection, and this former church building sit on the shared traditional territory of the Chonnonton, Anishnaabe and Haudenosaunee peoples. This land is part of the *Dish with One Spoon Treaty* between the Haudenosaunee and Anishnaabe peoples, symbolizing the agreement to share, to protect our resources and not to engage in conflict.

By the time St Mark's Lutheran Church was built, the land located at the corner of King and Green Streets had long ago been appropriated. The stories told here reflect attempts to share resources and not to engage in conflict; efforts to serve and protect the sacred humanity in each person. These efforts are also reflected in the current repurposing of the building as supportive housing. While we cannot turn back earlier acts of appropriation, we can pray that the path forward reflects our respect for what was taken without permission.

May these efforts serve as part of our heartfelt apology for sins of appropriation, and may the stories included here serve as a small measure of recognition that the world and its resources, including land, are never ours to keep, but to share with love and humility.

Rev. Janaki Bandara
with Rev. Rosalyn Kantlaht'ant Elm

Contents

Illustrations and Credits | xii
Acknowledgements | xv
Preface | xix

Advent, Christmas, and a Whisper of Epiphany | 1
In the Hall beside the Main Floor Washrooms | 3
The Porch Light's On! | 5
Feet | 9
Hands | 12
God is Innocent | 15
Down to Earth | 19
The Hockey Stick | 22

Transfiguration | 25
Behind the Scenes | 27

Lent, Holy Week, and Easter | 31
The Coffee Urn | 33
Poem: Sanctuary of the Impossible | 38
Holy Week | 39
Wounded Hands | 42
Fluffy Bath Towels | 45
The Gooseneck Lamp | 48
Poem: Wherever You Go | 51

Pentecost | 53

The Peace Garden | 55

Poem: Here Now | 61

The Laneway | 62

Across the Distance | 66

The Variety Store around the Corner | 71

Ordinary Time(s) | 75

Child by Child | 77

The Baptismal Font | 80

That One's Cracked!! | 83

Each Perfect Gift | 86

Poem: Wanted | 90

Sign Language | 92

Poem: Signage | 95

Something like Roses | 96

The Food Voucher Binder | 99

The Back Door | 104

Pink Paper Hearts | 107

Ballots | 110

The Phone in the Hall | 115

Kind-hearted Jesus | 118

Memo | 121

Endangered | 123

Saint Francis and the Farting Dog | 126

The Bowl of Mints | 129

The Crying Pew | 132

All Saints' Day | 135

The Procession | 137

Reign of Christ | 141

Tale of Two Crowns | 143

Small and Extravagant | 146

Postlude | 149

   Poem: Dear is the Ground | 152

Bibliography | 153

Illustrations and Credits

Fig. 1   In the Hall beside the Main Floor Washrooms | 3
Open hands. Photo by Andrew Moca (Unsplash.com)

Fig. 2   The Porch Light's On! | 5
Porch light. Photo by epiphanyvp (Pixabay.com)

Fig. 3   Feet | 9
Footprint in the snow. Photo by Chris F. (Pexels.com)

Fig. 4   Hands | 12
Clasped hands. Photo by Mirka (Pixabay.com)

Fig. 5   God is Innocent | 15
Bird's nest. Photo by Emma Schell (Unsplash.com)

Fig. 6   Down to Earth | 19
Incubator infant. Photo by Alexander Grey (Unsplash.com)

Fig. 7   The Hockey Stick | 22
Young hockey player. Photo by Jill Wellington (Pixabay.com)

Fig. 8   Behind the Scenes | 27
Table still-life. St. Mark's Archives, used with permission.

Fig. 9   The Coffee Urn | 33
Tea and coffee shelf. St. Mark's Archives, used with permission.

Fig. 10   Holy Week | 39
Tree of Life banner designed by Nancy-Lou Patterson, Grand River Hospital, Freeport Campus Chapel. Used with permission of the artist's family. Photo by the author.

Fig. 11   Wounded Hands | 42
Detail from resurrection banners designed by Nancy-Lou Patterson, now at Trillium Lutheran Church, Waterloo. Used with permission of St. Mark's Archives and artist's family.

Fig. 12   Fluffy Bath Towels | 45
Fluffy bath towel. St. Mark's Archives, used with permission.

Fig. 13   The Gooseneck Lamp | 48
Lectern light. St. Mark's Archives, used with permission.

Fig. 14   The Peace Garden | 55
Peace Garden. St. Mark's Archives, used with permission.

Fig. 15   The Peace Garden | 57

Fig. 16   The Laneway | 62
Church laneway. St. Mark's Archives, used with permission.

Fig. 17   Across the Distance | 66
World map hands. Photo by stokpic (Pixabay.com)

Fig. 18   The Variety Store around the Corner | 71
Neighborhood variety store. St. Mark's Archives, used with permission.

Fig. 19   Child by Child | 77
Nursing infant. Photo by анастасия-войтко (Pexels.com)

Fig. 20   The Baptismal Font | 80
Hands in the font. St. Mark's Archives, used with permission.

Fig. 21   That One's Cracked!! | 83
Stephen Ministry banner created by Helen Weber. St. Mark's Archives, used with permission.

Fig. 22   Each Perfect Gift | 86
Holding a sparkler. Photo by Jamie Street (Unsplash.com)

Fig. 23   Sign Language | 92
Bundled cutlery. Photo by Tim Douglas (Pexels.com)

Fig. 24   Something like Roses | 96
Rose bouquet detail. Photo by Jess Bailey Designs (Pexels.com)

Fig. 25   The Food Voucher Binder | 99
Kitchen still-life. St. Mark's Archives, used with permission.

Fig. 26 The Back Door | 104
Church back door. St. Mark's Archives, used with permission.

Fig. 27 Pink Paper Hearts | 107
Paper hearts and messages. St. Mark's Archives, used with permission.

Fig. 28 Ballots | 110
Ballot slips. St. Mark's Archives, used with permission. Clipart of couple from publicdomainvectors.org

Fig. 29 The Phone in the Hall | 115
Telephone and receiver. Photo by Vecteezy.com

Fig. 30 Kind-hearted Jesus | 118
Stained glass window of crucifixion. St. Mark's Archives, used with permission.

Fig. 31 Memo | 121
AA meeting sign. St. Mark's Archives, used with permission.

Fig. 32 Endangered | 123
Hand cradling a small bird. Photo by Nine Koepfer (Unsplash.com)

Fig. 33 St. Francis and the Farting Dog | 126
Euphonium. Photo by Janosch Diggelmann (Unsplash.com)

Fig. 34 The Bowl of Mints | 129
Mint bowl. St. Mark's Archives, used with permission.

Fig. 35 The Crying Pew | 132
Sun-dappled back pews. St. Mark's Archives, used with permission.

Fig. 36 The Procession | 137
Church center aisle. St. Mark's Archives, used with permission.

Fig. 37 Tale of Two Crowns | 143
Crowns of thorns and gold. Photo from https://static.wixstatic.com/media

Fig. 38 Small and Extravagant | 146
Mustard seed in palm. St. Mark's Archives, used with permission.

Fig. 39 St. Mark's Place
Under Construction, St. Mark's Place. St. Mark's Archives, used with permission.

Acknowledgements

To my family, my heart, my shelter, my dearest ones: to you Robert, my partner in life and in ministry. To you, our daughters Jana and Sara, and you, our grandchildren William and Hannah. All of you walked this journey with me. The best gift.

To those in the foreground and those in the background of these stories. You who like members of so many congregations mourned a past you cherished. You who asked hard questions and kept learning as you struggled with the direction of ministry in a time of so many changes. You who knocked on the door and bravely came inside. Your various hungers embodied the pulse of the Gospel at the corner of King and Green and beyond.

To Rev. Rebecca Yoder Neufeld. When I mentioned an earlier book I was writing, you said, "That's fine, but what I'm really looking forward to is reading the ministry stories you tell." Dear Becky, here they are!

To Rev. Janaki Bandara, with support from Rev. Rosalyn Kantlaht'ant Elm, for contributing the heartfelt Land Acknowledgment at the beginning of this book.

To Alan Totzke, the Archives Manager of the former St. Mark's Lutheran Church in Kitchener, Ontario, for your permission to publish archival photos in this book.

To Jennifer Schmidt for selecting and meticulously formatting the illustrations for this book, your labour of love.

To Patrick Rittinger, for your landscape design for The Peace Garden which still sparks joy.

To Sara Wahl for permission to publish your photo of the magical moment you jumped up on a pew during worship and took a picture of the children's hands and mine in the baptismal waters.

To Owen Roberts for your permission to publish photos of the one-of-a-kind baptismal bowl your mother Ann Roberts created for St. Mark's.

To Melanie Wawryk and your family for permission to share photos of your mother Nancy-Lou Patterson's beautiful banners.

To Dr. Benjamin Lefebvre and Jacob Letkemann for permission to share the meditation from your wedding.

To Marilyn Burnard and the Community Ministry Management Committee of Calvary Memorial United Church and the former St. Mark's Lutheran Church for your permission to re-publish stories and a poem I wrote for "See You Next Week: An Ecumenical Community Ministry in an Ontario Downtown."

To Jim Oakley for permission to share your photo of the transformation of St. Mark's Lutheran Church into St. Mark's Place.

To Diane Bonfonte for providing archival information about the opening service of St. Mark's.

To my earliest readers. Your thoughtful feedback, questions, suggestions and encouragement helped shape my telling of these stories: Sarah and Rev. Ken Cardwell, Rev. Claudine Carlson, Rev. Katherine Gohm, Lilla Hall, Rev. Dr. Robert Kelly, Rev. Dr. Stephen Larson, Rev. John Lougheed, Dr. Rebekah Ludolph, Dr. Laura MacGregor, Robin Pearson, Bishop Michael Pryse, Mary Slethaug, and Dr. Mary Thompson.

To my mentors in faith, especially the children of St. Mark's and many friends from El Salvador. You opened many hearts, including mine, to thrilling ways of reading the Bible and being the church. You are among my best teachers.

To Pastor Philip Mathai and the people of Mount Zion Lutheran Church in Waterloo, Ontario. You nurtured my faith and vocation while I was writing this book.

To beloved colleagues at St. Mark's: Pastor Fred and Debbie Lou Ludolph, Pastor Elizabeth Kuglin-Alyea, Pastor Vern and Bette Cronmiller, Rev. Dr. Harold Remus, Rev. Dr. Cindy Jacobsen and Rev. Dr. David Jacobsen, Rev. Dr. Peter and Myra Van Katwyk, Rev. Jim and Wilma Marie Bindernagel, Rev. Marilyn and Tom Burnard, Lilla and David Hall, Holly Mathers, Rowene Harlock, Cheryl Melnyk, Nancy MacLean, the Holst family and countless seminary field placement students. And to beloved colleagues next door and around the corner for the creative, supportive partnership we shared across laneways and parking lots, in church kitchens and parish halls, at the hospital and in the high school: Rev. John Lougheed, Lila Read, Patrick Rittinger and Juanita Harrington.

To the pastors and people of Trillium Lutheran Church, Waterloo, for your support in telling these stories. And to Monica Scheifele for your open-hearted ministry of hospitality.

To Pauline Finch, you first read these stories one at a time, slowly, devotionally, then patiently and gently read them over and over and over again to help lead them to publication. Your grasp of ministry and meanings, attentiveness to detail and love for Christ's church infuse every page of this book.

Preface

"There are stories that cannot be silenced.
There are stories that are stronger than death.
There are stories that can raise us from our fears."[1]

MARTY HAUGEN
"SONG OF MARK"

Ancient mapmakers had a striking way of identifying how scary it can be when the present time is unsettled, the future is uncertain, and we're not sure which way to turn. At the edge of the known world, these mapmakers sometimes warned: "Here be dragons."[2] In other words, "No guarantee of safe passage. If you want to avoid the hazards, back off."

For followers of Jesus, here's another possibility; when (*not if!*) we near the end of what we know. Through the eyes of faith, we can see Christ out ahead of us on the map, arms outstretched, beckoning us forward. While Jesus warns us about dangers, at the same time he always "call[s] from tomorrow"[3] urging us forward into uncharted waters through the dangers, disappointments, disillusionments, doubts and discouragements. His map,

1. Marty Haugen, "Here Begins the Good News" from "Song of Mark." Chicago: GIA Publications, 1996.

2. National Geographic Society, "Here Be Dragons." https://education. nationalgeographic.org/resource/here-be-dragons Retrieved August 11, 2022.

3. James K. Manley, "Spirit, Spirit of Gentleness," text of Hymn No. 396, *Evangelical Lutheran Worship*. Minneapolis: Augsburg Fortress, 2006.

in goodness and mercy, embraces transformation through life, death, and resurrection.

This adventurous, unpredictable part of God's ways draws me to tell you these stories. When glimpses of God's wonders reveal something about the limits of our own vision, and about our power and privilege, or our *lack* of power and privilege, these hints can certainly be disruptive. They might cause us to say, "We didn't sign up for this." Yet these times and these ways also have the power to reveal truths we don't quite understand—and don't want to. Truths about ourselves and our neighbors near and far. Truths about the future shape of ministry. Truths to unpack about God and God's radical grace.

The nerve! God acts without consulting us and our strategic plans. God acts in ways we find alarming and bewildering. God acts in ways that mess with the status quo. Ways that aren't what we were hoping for. Ways that have the power to re-shape us and re-orient us.

Stories about these times and these ways matter.[4] They carry the steady pulse of God's goodness and mercy. This collection of stories is testimony to the wonder of new life springing up in a particular group of ordinary, vulnerable, flesh-and-blood beings, human people in a changing Christian congregation. Yet stories like these are always happening, to everyone, everywhere, whether we're paying attention or not. Even when we're on the way to somewhere else. I experienced and/or witnessed these stories when I was a pastor of St. Mark's Lutheran Church in Kitchener, Ontario from 1995 to 2013.[5] Those years were a time of much change as we lived with neighbors near and far within the embrace of God's big love.

4. Richard Kearney, *On Stories: Thinking in Action.* (New York: Routledge & Francis Group, 2002), 14, 125. Chapter "Narrative Matters."

5. In 2018, the people of St. Mark's Lutheran Church made the bold decision to amalgamate with two other local congregations to form Trillium Lutheran Church in Waterloo, Ontario. https://trilliumwaterloo.ca/. The building once consecrated as St. Mark's Lutheran Church closed and has now become St. Mark's Place to provide 43 units of supportive housing sponsored by Indwell. https://indwell.ca/st-marks-place. Visited October 10, 2022

I see myself as a steward of these stories, and telling them now is my way of fleshing out a much bigger story. Though a particular beloved place and people are, necessarily, at the heart of these "Word made flesh," incarnational stories, I invite you to listen deeply, beyond that particular place, to what these stories reveal about the wild, untamed grace of God. My intent as a storyteller is to encourage you to contemplate what God might be saying to us about God and about the present and future of the church.

In these stories, unforeseen consequences arise in the middle of life both scripted and not. In interruptions and improbabilities, inherited expectations are turned upside-down challenging what we thought we knew and believed. I collected these stories here for you, trusting that they have the potential to generate new life in ministry when we ask each other what they might be revealing to us about God's imagination. The church and dare I say the world need you to tell your own wonder stories as we face the certainty of new "ventures of which we cannot see the ending, by paths as yet untrodden, through perils unknown."[6]

Krista Tippett, host of the American National Public Radio series "On Being," first opened my eyes to what she calls "the moral potential of surprise."[7] In these stories, sometimes the *moral* potential of surprise includes the *mortal* potential of surprise—evidence of the life-giving potential to help heal society's deadly devaluation of life and the divisions that cause mortal injury to human beings and all of God's creation.

I trust you won't be surprised to hear that I am both drawn to and wary of the wild, untamed grace of God. I surely don't recognize wonder in every moment and movement of ministry! These stories are about the times in community when I did, by grace, perceive that wonder, was moved by it and among those who were transformed.

6. *Evangelical Lutheran Worship*. Minneapolis: Augsburg Fortress, 2006. Service of Morning Prayer (Matins), 304.

7. Krista Tippet, "On Being" newsletter, "The Pause." January 8, 2022. https://onbeing.org/newsletter/.

When we're off the known map, a sense of wonder that comes as a gift from God is worthy of proclaiming in our own voices. That's when, in spite of ourselves and when we least expect it, we're living under the influence of resurrection—even when fear and death make so much more sense.

Nancy Vernon Kelly

Advent, Christmas, and a Whisper of Epiphany

A dvent, Christmas, and Epiphany start off the Church Year by giving us a time to pause and ponder an infinitely provocative contradiction. We await the arrival of someone who is already here with us.

In these first stories, now in your hands, a gift-giver places a little unexpected gift in my hands. Then, a modern-day pied piper will lead us to a house on a sad and frightened street. As we live in the space between darkness and light, the power of God in Christ, beyond all reason, will shine within the darkness—even in "the valley of the shadow of death."

Then, at a downtown transit terminal, in the midst of humanity on the go, a travelling man reveals what a gift it is, right now, that Christ is afoot where we are walking and also where we will go next. On the top floor of a long-term care center, we will pause at the intersection of wounded hands, within the poignancy of loneliness and relationship—especially at Christmastime. Arriving at the church building, a small group of worshipers will proclaim God's glory in their own voices. God is with us. God is innocent. And God loves everybody.

Finally, we will arrive at a surprising place where incarnation and Christmas gift-giving meet.

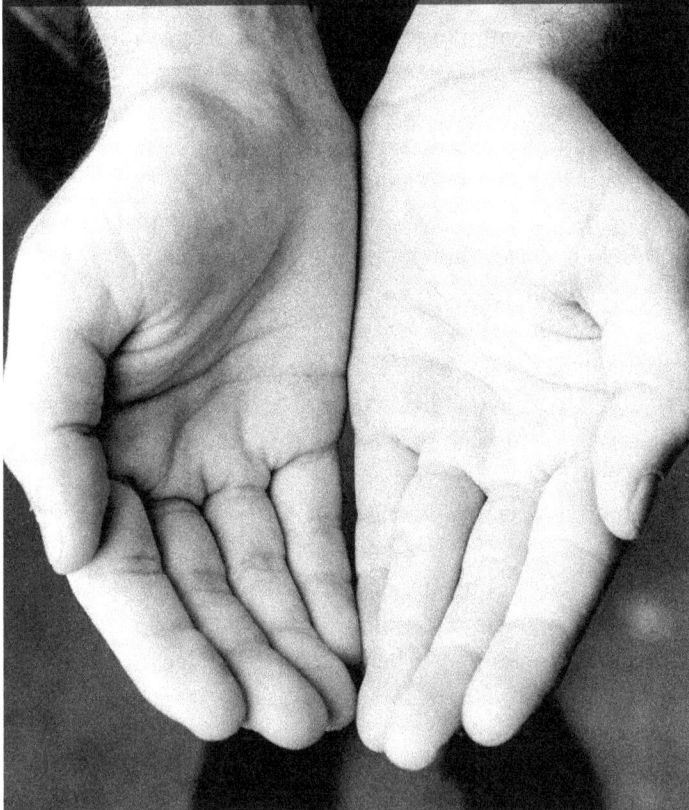

In the Hall Beside the Main Floor Washrooms

"The word became flesh and lived among us."

JOHN 1:14[1]

1. *NRSV.*

L ate one Wednesday afternoon shortly before Christmas, inside an old, heart-of-the-city brick church, one of the regulars was finishing off a cup of coffee from the coffee shop next door. She had arrived early to help prepare the turkeys and all the fixings for the community supper and chit-chat with friends. She startled me when we bumped into each other, literally, in the hall beside the main floor washroom. What more down-to-earth place than that? I was preoccupied, hurried, on the way from one place to another. I surely wasn't looking for revelation.

Yet revelation was looking for me. Suddenly, there the woman was. In my face. Actually, in the flesh in my face, grinning like a big smiley emoji.

"Open your hand," the woman insisted. "This is for you."

Though, at first, I felt wary of the woman's closed fist and what it might contain, I held out both hands, forming them into a little manger—the way someone long ago said that Martin Luther taught worshipers to do when we receive Communion.

Into my open hands, the woman dropped a stained, crumpled coupon good for a free coffee at Tim Hortons, one of the most popular coffee and doughnut places in town; Tim Hortons just happened to have an outlet in the hospital lobby next door to the church. The woman ripped her offering from her own paper coffee cup and presented it to me.

Once long ago, Jesus arrived in our face. And he's still arriving in our face now to show us our place in the universe. To challenge our assumptions and fire our imaginations. To nourish our individual and communal lives and to restore our hope. To help us join with God and with others, in flesh and blood ways, to renew the face of the earth. I hope you will welcome this first story and the stories that follow. Open your hand. This is for you.

The Porch Light's On!

"Within our darkest night, you kindle the fire that never dies away."

TAIZÉ COMMUNITY[1]

1. Communauté de Taizé. "Within Our Darkest Night." (Les Presses de Taizé, GIA Publications Inc. agent), 1991.

T hat year the Fourth Sunday in Advent came two days after the longest night of the year and one day short of the first full moon of winter. With a flash freeze warning on the news, patches of ice on the ground, flurries of snow in the air, and a bitter wind blowing through bare trees, a group of us went caroling. Among us we had been caroling many times before, in hospitals and long-term care centers, on many streets, in front of many houses, in many cities.

And this year's carolling was like none other.

Days before, a spirit of gloom descended on the community after a local man was murdered in broad daylight on a street near his home as he delivered Christmas cards to his neighbors. We all knew his name from news reports, and we all knew the saddest and most disturbing part of this story.

A church member who'd heard about the tragedy was so touched by the pain inflicted on the murdered man's family that he stood up during announcements on Sunday morning and appealed to people to go carolling with him on the dead man's street.

At half-past six, barely recognizable in toques, hoods, scarves and coats, a group of about forty carollers arrived in a neighborhood where the sidewalks and the front yards and the houses and the street itself looked safe. Before we turned the corner, the pied piper gathered us into a circle. He reminded us that we couldn't end the grief on this street. What we could do was bring a little flicker of hope and warmth to the people who lived there to let them know they weren't alone. In that spirit, he led us down the middle of the street where the bereaved family lived. The street where an innocent husband and father and neighbor had senselessly died.

While we walked, we sang traditional Christmas carols that contain repeated references to both night and day. Words like "Yet in thy dark streets shineth the everlasting light"[2] rang especially

2. Text: Phillips Brooks, 1835-1893. Music: Lewis H. Redner, 1831-1908. "O Little Town of Bethlehem." Public Domain. *Evangelical Lutheran Worship*. Minneapolis: Augsburg Fortress, 2006. No. 279.

true that night. Singing theses familiar words gave chills that had nothing to do with the weather.

As we approached the man's house, whispers rippled through the group. *This* is the place. *This* is the house. The day before, when the gentle pied piper let the family know we were coming, he learned that the man's widow wasn't staying there. Yet, when we arrived, the porch light was on! A beacon in the gloom. And there she was, standing in the driveway by the street, surrounded by family members who brought her home to hear the carols. Not only did her family come home with her, they were singing along with the church carollers as were some of the neighbors who had heard the singing and come out on their porches.

Naturally, the group sang "Silent Night," which the deceased man's family and friends had also sung the day before at his funeral. Two days after the longest night of the year and one day short of the first full moon of winter, carollers and neighbors and the grieving family affirmed: "Son of God, love's pure light, radiance beams from his holy face, with the dawn of redeeming grace." The juxtaposition of "the dawn of redeeming grace"[3] with the horror of the man's murder was jarring, unforgettable. And at the same time, the act of singing together sparked a sense of communal sorrow-bearing in deepest night.

That night revealed a small, substantial and comforting hint of the dawn from on high that God promises will break upon humanity, shining on all of us who live within the shadow of death and at the same time guiding our feet into a community of peace.[4]

Does the light of Christ still shine in the deepest night even when dark clouds obscure the almost full moon? A hint of an answer comes in the intersection of the words of an ancient Christmas carol, a broken-hearted family who showed up anyway, a bright porch light, and a group of bundled up carollers. Where

3. German Text: Joseph Mohr, 1792-1849. English trans: John F. Young, 1820-1885. Music: Franz Gruber, 1787-1863. Public Domain. *Evangelical Lutheran Worship*. Minneapolis: Augsburg Fortress, 2006. No. 281.

4. Luke 1:76. Adapted from the *NRSV*.

the light of Christ fills the hearts of God's people, that light still shines even in the "valley of the shadow of death."

And who knows? Given that the light of Christ is God's power, it wouldn't be surprising to hear that someone was also proclaiming in song "the dawn of redeeming grace" on the street where the man's assailant and his family lived. And in the jail where he was being held. And in all the hopeless places close by and around the world that are convinced that all the light had gone out. Places where people desperately needed reassurance of something more than they could see, places where the faithful pulse of God's goodness and mercy was channeled through flesh-and-blood companions on the journey.

Sometimes, beyond all reason, sorrow and wonder rendezvous.

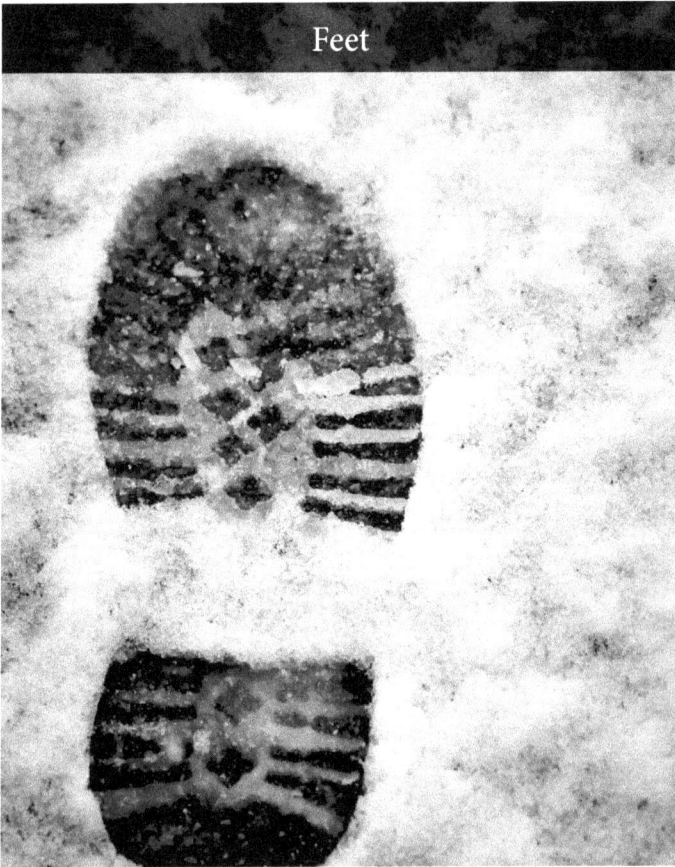

Feet

"Crucifixion was not the hard part for Christ. Incarnation was."

ALISON HAWTHORNE DEMING[1]

1. Deming, Alison Hawthorne. "Resurrection." *Columbia Daily Tribune,* September 20, 2016. https://www.columbiatribune.com/story/entertainment/arts/2016/09/20/resurrection/21841879007. Retrieved August 29, 2022.

I never knew his name or his story. I knew him through his feet, through the steps he took. He was one man among crowds of people, day after day pacing back and forth on the main floor of the downtown transit terminal. Twelve paces toward Charles Street. Twelve paces toward Victoria School on Joseph Street. The same twelve paces, over and over again, hour after hour, day after day, cutting across the path of busy humanity.[2]

He could have been anywhere on earth, but that day it happened that he was in the same place as I was. So, I saw him. I heard the sound of his footsteps. He was among us. If you were there, you would have seen him too, crossing your path. Twelve paces toward Victoria School. Twelve paces back toward Charles Street.

Just before Christmas, when shuttling between home communion visits, I watched the pacing man as I waited for the city bus. As I watched, I also wondered. Who was he? What was his story? And how would he tell it? He wasn't bothering anybody, and nobody seemed to be bothering him. Once in a while, when he bumped into someone or someone bumped into him, one or the other just stepped aside to make way.

The man had a purpose I couldn't see. His was no aimless meander. There was a rhythm to his walk. Before long, in that place filled with hurry and rush, in a season filled with hurry and rush, in a community filled with hurry and rush, I began to slow down, breathing to the rhythm of his footsteps, breathing to the sound of his heavy boots shuffling across the slushy floor in a certain, reassuring cadence. Twelve steps toward Victoria School. A smooth pivot on one foot. Twelve steps back toward Charles Street.

As I sat there watching him, a flood of questions welled up. Who was this man? Could he be a little glimpse of "the Word made flesh . . . dwelling among us full of grace and truth?" If so, what was he saying? If he was a glimpse of Emmanuel, God with us, he was silently walking in the places we walk, very humanly present, cutting across the common pathways of life, making holy every speck

2. Nancy Vernon Kelly, based on "The word became a human being" in "Consensus: A Canadian journal of public theology", 2001. http://scholars.wlu.ca/consensus/vol27/iss2/10. Retrieved December 10, 2021.

of the ground he walked on. By his presence was he marking the ground *we* walk on as holy too? If he was Emmanuel, he was at risk of getting cancer and diabetes and becoming displaced. Of finding no help for his mental health needs. If he was a glimpse of Emmanuel, he was certainly at risk (considerable risk) of slobbering, as a child once blurted out during a children's sermon on Christmas Eve. Which led other children to talk about incarnation in terms of sneezing, gurgling, cooing and, of course, burping.

This particular man left his mark, making holy footprints in a common place filled with travelling humanity. He was out of order, intrusive, not playing by the accepted rules. Hmmm. From then on, for the rest of the day, whenever I caught a glimpse of feet walking through the snow, or on the pavement, or on a well-worn carpet, the same crux-of-the-matter question returned. What if *this* one, this one crossing my path right now, this one beside me, is a glimpse of the One who is making holy the ground beneath my feet and everyone else's feet, too?

When Christ haunts the world with his presence, there's nowhere on earth where he isn't pacing back and forth, looking at us intently, his brow knitted with concern, or perhaps with a big smile on his face, marking each place as holy, a place where he has chosen to be. Not just in church sanctuaries. *Everywhere* he chooses to walk. God with us. A human being pleased to be at home inside human skin and to experience the joy and sorrow of being human. One of us.

One of the countless places where God in Christ wears a disguise and hides is a downtown transit terminal in the midst of travelling humanity. Other common places he walks are everywhere today beyond the walls of churches, the same places we are walking now and the places where we will go next.

Hands

"We were holding hands as hands were holding us."

DAVID BAKER[1]

1. David Baker, "On Hands," *New York Times*, November 18, 2021. https://www.nytimes.com/2021/11/18/magazine/poem-hold-hands.htm. Retrieved March 30, 2022.

T his story unfolded in the place where I went next on the public bus on that cold December afternoon just before Christmas. The place where a dignified white-haired woman in a top floor room of a long-term care center was talking with me about the meaning of life. In particular, she was considering the meaning of her own very long life. A life of increasing dependence. A life of diminishing possibilities. A life of sighing.

The woman wondered aloud what possible use she could be, trapped there in her wheelchair, on the other end of town from her beloved clapboard home on a tree-lined street. In the long-term care center, she might as well have been in a foreign country. Another world. No kitchen to bake pies in. No garden to tend. No bay window to polish until it sparkled.

This story is about the conversation that started while an improvised communion table was prepared on her footstool. The bread. The wine. The little battery-operated candle. The meal could wait while she poured out her heart.

She remembered one recent evening among many when she was wheeling herself from the dining room back into her room, where the single bed was made up with her own quilt, and close by were her television, her closet, and some shelves holding a few keepsakes. Her window looked out on a bowling alley and pizza parlor, where she could watch much younger people coming and going.

On her way back to her room that evening, she passed by the Christmas tree and admired the lights and festive evergreen garlands, feeling wistful. She noticed another resident, an elderly man also in a wheelchair, lined up with several others along the wall. In fact, she'd seen him there every day, the same blank, deadened look on his face.

That evening, not stopping to think about it, the woman spontaneously reached out and gently patted the old man's hand. She just reached out and touched him. And as soon as she did, he suddenly came alive, gripping her hand so tightly in return she thought it might break. If a string quartet had been accompanying the moment, the composer's guidance would have been *Animato,* lively. Calling to life. His hand and also hers.

When the woman told this story, she was sitting by the window in her upstairs room. As she finished, a long moment of silence followed, making room for us to be "present to the presence" as Father Richard Rohr[2] would say. Present to the Presence with a capital P. That Presence was wondrous, palpable in the room, *with* us, for even as she told the story, we were already sharing communion.

2. Richard Rohr, "Being Present to the Presence of God." (Center for Action and Contemplation, 2021). https://cac.org/daily-meditations/being-present-to-the-presence-of-god-2021-11-12/. Retrieved July 18, 2022.

God is Innocent

*"It's . . . as if Someone was building Eternity as
a swallow its nest out of clumps of moments."*

ANNA KAMIEŃSKA[1]

1. Anna Kamieńska. "Small Things" in *Astonishments, Selected Poems of
Anna Kamieńska.* (Brewster: Paraclete, 2007), 45. Trans. 2007 by Grażyna
Drabik and David Curzon.

A few days before Christmas, about twenty people gathered in the north transept of the old city church. Everyone else had gone home. The community Christmas supper in the Parish Hall was finished, and we were all stuffed with turkey, dressing and all the trimmings.[2]

The traditional Service of Lessons and Carols was just about to begin when a woman in the front row yelled out, "That's a *big tree*. But there's no ornaments on it!" Wide-eyed, she pointed to the enormous pine a family had cut down on their farm to give to the church. All that hung on its branches were many strands of tiny, sparkling white lights.

I explained that we were waiting. It was still Advent, the week before Christmas. At the right time, the youth group would decorate the tree. The woman was taking it all in and at the same time waiting patiently for another turn to speak. Not satisfied, she jumped in again, "If I make an odd ornament can I hang it on the tree?"

"Sure," I said, wondering if I was telling the truth or a lie.

Soon most of us—a collection of God's odd ornaments—were singing "O Come, O Come, Emmanuel" *a capella* because the guitarist hadn't shown up. "Is that like Acapulco?" the woman asked. "Could be," I answered.

I don't think it's an exaggeration to say that each of us was mourning "in lonely exile" in our own ways on that snowy night, waiting for God to appear. Since we were on the cusp of Christmas, one among us stood up at the front and read the Christmas story from Luke:

> In that region there were shepherds living in the fields, keeping watch over their flock by night. Then an angel of the Lord stood before them, and the glory of the Lord shone around them, and they were terrified. But the angel said to them, 'Do not be afraid; for see—I am bringing you good news of great joy for all the people: to you is born this day in the city of David a Saviour, who is the

2. Nancy Vernon Kelly, "God is Innocent," in *See You Next Week: An Ecumenical Community Ministry in an Ontario Downtown*. Marilyn Shaw, Harold Remus and Nancy Kelly, eds. (Kitchener, ON: Community Ministry, 2007), 105. Reprinted with permission.

*Messiah, the Lord. This will be a sign for you: you will find
a child wrapped in bands of cloth and lying in a manger
. . . The shepherds returned, glorifying and praising God
for all they had heard and seen, as it had been told them.*[3]

In response to the reading of the Gospel, I lifted up a soft-bodied baby doll and asked if anybody knew what "Emmanuel" meant. Very quietly the guy in a baseball cap said, "God with us." If I hadn't already known the answer, I'm not sure I would have heard it. And he was right. "Emmanuel"—God with us.

I placed the baby doll in a woman's arms and handed her the soft knit blanket borrowed from the Knitting Tree, a big branch covered with caps, mitts and blankets destined for a local women's shelter. The woman was shy about the whole thing, embarrassed at being singled out to hold the baby.

"It's been a long time," she said, looking down and gently swaddling the Baby Jesus. She held him so close to her heart a live baby would have felt her warmth and heard her heart beating. With a collective sigh, everyone quieted down.

Why do you think God decided to be born as a baby? That was the starter question that night. And each took a turn holding Baby Jesus as we answered, each in our own way.

The first answer came from a man I'd never seen before. "To show us God is innocent." His words were important and repeatable. "To show us God is innocent."

There we were. Damaged. Each one tossed and turned by the ocean of life. And sad over one thing or another. Somebody missed her kids. Somebody felt anxious. Somebody else felt left out. Somebody didn't have anywhere to spend the night, and it was very cold outside. One woman wasn't sure about this Baby and told us so.

All had experienced guilt and innocence . . . our own and other people's. As if we were in a courtroom, the jury had just met, and it was now time to announce the verdict, we heard the words: "God is innocent." For heaven's sake, God is a little baby and a baby can't be responsible for making us or anybody else mad, or violent, or

3. Luke 2:8-12, 20. *NRSV.*

mean-spirited, or proud, or greedy, or depressed, or resentful, or abused, or addicted, or poor, or hungry, or any of the other bad things we blame God for. The verdict was clear: "God is innocent."

The innocent Baby Jesus was passed to a man who shared something that was bothering him. Something that was so hard to understand. He was far from home and never had any children of his own. He was pretty sure nobody would ever trust him with a baby. And Baby Jesus was right up close, nuzzling his rough face, listening.

Another man had parked his wheelchair in the aisle cut-out. "God decided to become a baby because God loves everybody like a baby loves everybody." And he went on to talk very quietly about how some people make fun of others and how some people made fun of Jesus, too. This man had the authority of experience. It was hard for him to get the words out, yet he knew what he was talking about. Many were nodding. I was listening as well as I could, repeating every word just to make sure we all got it. Because the words were important.

Meanwhile, by then, Baby Jesus was sleeping out of the cold in somebody else's arms. That night everybody wanted their turn to be the place where he was born. To hold him so close he could hear their heart beating . . . to be his manger.

After the benediction a fellow in overalls waited until no one else was around and asked me a riddle. "Who's closer to a hillbilly? A hippy or a redneck?" I guessed the redneck, and got it wrong.

"Nope," he said with gentle confidence. He knew he had me. "Neither one." His eyes twinkling, he explained "The hillbilly's a bridge between the two . . . a bridge between the hippy and the redneck."

By then the candles were out and the man in overalls and I stood together in the dim church. "Say, thanks for repeating everything tonight," he said. "Usually I miss a lot, and I could hear almost everything."

"I did it for all of us," I said. "I usually miss a lot, too."

Then the man in overalls bent down and whispered something wondrous in my one pretty good ear: "This is the first time I ever held a baby."

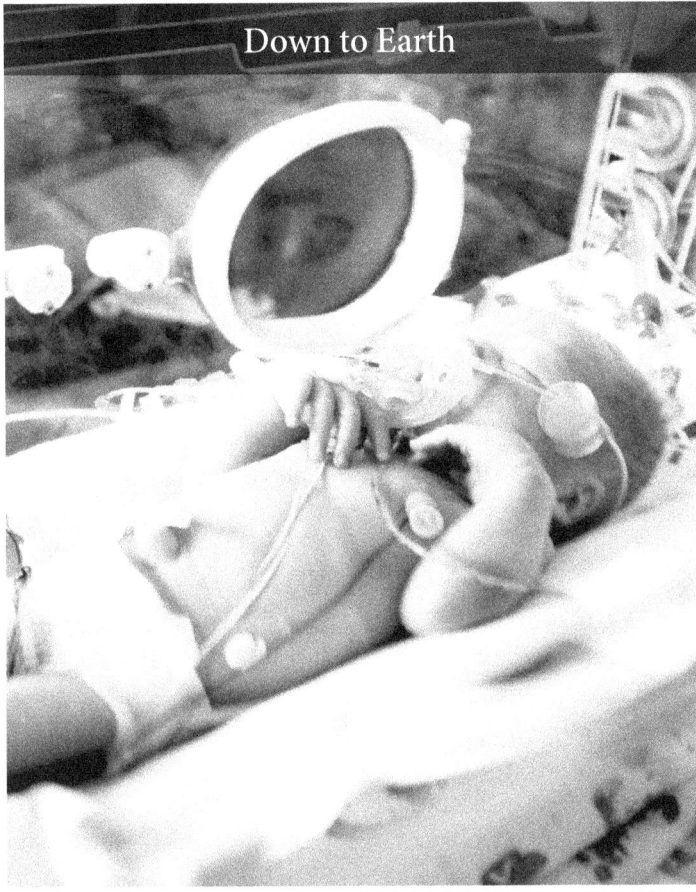

Down to Earth

"The feelings [awe] can elicit are best understood as a paradox: the sensation of feeling enriched by way of feeling diminished."

HENRY WISMAYER[1]

---

1. See Wismayer, Henry, "Why Space Tourists Won't Find the Awe they Seek," *New York Times*, November 27, 2021. Retrieved August 10, 2022. https://www.nytimes.com/2021/11/27/opinion/space-tourism-awe.html.

This story is about another evening service days before Christmas Eve, another year. That year the Very Particular Baby was a doll with a smudge on his face. He was soft-bodied, brown-skinned, made-in-China, wrapped in a prayer shawl, and lying in a laundry basket. Before the service, someone filled up the basket with a pile of kiddy kits (destined for world relief) to raise the baby high enough so everybody could see.

On that bitterly cold December night, attendance at worship after the community supper was, as always, unpretentious. Five at the start. Maybe fifteen of us by the benediction. After enjoying our annual free community Christmas supper, with roast turkey donated by a local farmer and little gifts for everybody, our tummies were full.

But this didn't mean all was well.

Even before the service started, with the organ prelude playing quietly in the background, a woman in the front row was telling the group how miserable she was, trying to warm up. Earlier in the week she had spent the night on a chilly church floor. "Don't worry about me being homeless," she said, waving her hands in the air as if to shoo away a bad vibe. "It's a temporary thing. Something always turns up."

And with this unguarded grace note during the prelude, the little service began.

A pair of angelic singers sang a duet. Then, one among us read the Christmas story including the Epiphany part about the ones who tiptoed inside the barn, saw Baby Jesus in Mother Mary's arms, and fell to their knees, filled with reverent joy. There they worshiped Jesus and opened up their treasure chests to offer their best gifts in thanksgiving: gold, frankincense, and myrrh.

"Once in a while," I began, "a baby is born at risk." I was standing in front of the woman who said she was still feeling cold. "Like a few weeks ago at the hospital next door, when a baby was born with a broken heart." Well, I could tell that many started paying closer attention when they heard about the baby born with a broken heart. Who doesn't know about broken hearts?

The question that night was this: "What would you give a baby at risk?"

And as the soft, made-in-China baby with spikey hair and crooked little smile was passed from person to person, some of the answers were predictable. Milk. Health. Warmth. Love. Then the sanctuary became very quiet before the angelic duet-singers looked at each other and smiled as they said they wanted to give the baby the gift of music. This broke the proverbial piñata wide open, and the treasures started pouring out.

The singing duo passed the baby to a grandfather who wanted to give him wisdom—the ability to discern right from wrong.

A grandmother across the aisle spoke next. She knew just how to hold the baby up next to her heart. "I'd babysit him for the afternoon to give his mother a break."

"I'd give him courage," the newcomer in a wheelchair said. "He's gonna need courage when he goes to the cross."

"A rod and a staff," another woman added with conviction. "I'd give him a rod and a staff."

Hmm, I thought. We're off the map. Where's this going? The woman's answer both intrigued and floored me. "A rod and a staff?"

"You'd give the baby a rod and a staff?"

"Well, it should be obvious," she said, sounding annoyed. "He needs a rod and a staff to help him lead us and guide us and keep us in the fold. Some folks think a rod and staff are harsh," she went on. "But a shepherd needs a rod and a staff to keep the sheep in line. We're willing to be led; it's just that the shepherd needs tools like a rod and a staff to keep us together. Especially when we start wandering. The Baby will need a rod and a staff to bring us back in."

Whew! Two more gifts for Baby Jesus: a rod and a staff to go along with food, warmth, love, music, wisdom, babysitting, and courage. Not exactly gold, frankincense, and myrrh. The little flock had offered one another an enlightening bend in the narrative of the story and stayed true to the basics.

The Hockey Stick

"The hint half guessed, the gift half understood, is Incarnation."

T.S. ELIOT[1]

1. T.S. Eliot, "Dry Salvages," in *Four Quartets,* (Boston: Mariner Books 1943), copyright renewed 1971 by Esme Valerie Eliot. 44.

One Sunday in Adult Education, the group sitting in a circle in the Church Parlor heard that Jesus probably had head lice because just about everybody in the time of Jesus had head lice. At the time, we were pondering the infinitely challenging revelation that Jesus was both God and human. How could that be? That's how the subject of dreaded head lice came up in church on Sunday morning.

One morning soon after, a man surprised me by rounding the corner at the top of the stairs and fairly leaping into my study. The man, well-known for posing the hardest of questions, asked, "Do you know if the boy who asked for a hockey stick is right- or left-handed?"

Since it was Advent, besides talking about head lice, we were in the middle of gathering up Christmas gifts for the "Spirit of Giving Tree" that stood in front of the church. It was decorated with handmade paper ornaments inscribed with gift requests from children and adults in our community.

When the gifts came into the church on Sundays and during the week, they piled up behind closed doors in my office until they were ready to be wrapped and delivered. Week by week, these gifts seemed to multiply in a corner by a bookcase—envelopes with gift certificates for supermarkets, teddy bears, pajamas, shampoo and bath towels. It was a joy to watch them coming in, some with tender-hearted handwritten Christmas greetings attached.

The man's hockey stick question was about one of the gifts destined for a child on Christmas morning. I didn't even know there *were* right- and left-handed hockey sticks, and I offered to call up the boy's mother and ask.

Later that same day, as I dialed the phone, there was one specific moment when I realized for sure that—along with head lice, wax in his ears, two big toes and a belly button—Jesus, unless he was ambidextrous, must have been right- or left-handed.

Which was it? Well, the bible doesn't answer that question. What we do know is that Jesus had hands.

These musings were interrupted when the boy's mother answered the phone. After chatting for a few minutes, I asked if her son was right- or left-handed. She told me that this particular fragment of the face of God—this child who longed for a hockey stick—was not a nameless entity, but a particular right-handed flesh-and-blood boy who was hoping for a hockey stick and some other children to play hockey with.

Fast forward a couple of weeks. A pile of straw had been added next to the mound of presents, parked there waiting to fill the manger at the front of the church for the family service on Christmas Eve. More gifts that had arrived for the "Spirit of Giving Tree" were waiting atop the straw to be wrapped and delivered. And there, in full view lying in the manger, I saw a brand new, right-handed hockey stick—in answer to a boy's deep human longing to be known and loved by others. Which is among the most beautiful, powerful, and wondrous ways we know we are known and loved by God. To be known and loved by others in our common humanity. And to be known and loved by others in our endless particularities.

Transfiguration

The story about the glorious transfiguration of Jesus holds his gritty down-to-earth ministry and his up-in-the-clouds brilliance in uneasy tension. Jesus, on his way to somewhere else—the cross—hikes up to a mountaintop with his disciples. There, he gets all sparkly and then comes God's clear endorsement: "This is my Son, the Beloved, with whom I am well pleased."[1] The disciples are eager to pitch some tents and camp out there on the mountaintop with Jesus, but he tells them they will have to leave that place and return to the pollution, commotion and communion of city streets and dusty roads. He doesn't give them a choice!

Jesus' transfiguration is a good place to pause before we move on to Lent and Easter. I'll lead you now to the big conference table in the church library to remember and give thanks to God for the messiness of ministry. The ups and downs. The loose ends. The unanswered questions. The heated discussions. The panic we feel when life is changing too fast in the world, in the church, in ourselves, and in those around us. The story of the transfiguration gives us the opportunity to remember and give thanks for the glitter that followers of Jesus occasionally catch a glimpse of.

Along the way, we often make a mess of things.

---

1. Matthew 3:17. *NRSV*.

Behind the Scenes

"The Love that dances at the heart of things
Shone out upon us from a human face."

MALCOLM GUITE[1]

---

1. Malcolm Guite, "A Sonnet on the Transfiguration" in *"Sounding the Seasons"* (London: Canterbury). https://malcolmguite.wordpress.com/2022/08/06/a-sonnet-on-the-transfiguration-3. Retrieved August 28, 2022.

T he big conference table in the church library was covered in microphones and rainbow baptismal candles and certificates and the missal and bulletins and sparkly glitter from the welcome cards Sunday School kids made for new members. Joyful energy was rising up from the people of God as we made a circle around that table. I loved that energy!

My colleague loved the energy too. He was presiding that morning, flying around in his shirt sleeves and blue Guatemalan vest . . . checking with the Music Director one last time . . . making sure there was water at the font . . . all the parents and sponsors had arrived and been seated . . . the acolyte could reach the candles and the assisting minister knew how to pronounce all the names in the prayers . . . there was oil for the anointing. Oops, there wasn't any oil for the anointing. So, he asked me to go and find some.

When I returned to the library with the oil, he was doing that little dance he did when wiggling into his long white alb. "We learned this in seminary," he announced, loud enough for the choir and worship leaders to hear. For a brief moment the hood was on his head, then off again, before his stole and chasuble were in place. Then he sighed a downward scale to "Shall we pray?" And he prayed in a way that left us smiling.

Soon we were lined up in the hall ready to go in. Then, what was that? What was he saying about *another* candle? One that belonged to the great grandmother of one of the baptismal babies? "Would you?" he said in sign language, gesturing to grab the candle-lighter.

By then he was off toward the end of the hall, turning on the PA system, leading the way into the nave of the church. I grabbed the candle lighter, bringing up the rear of the parade just in time for an acolyte to light the treasured old baptismal candle and pass the flame to the hands of the infant's grandmother. And in a moment pregnant with past, present, and future—life, death, and resurrection—the grandmother reverently lit her mother's baptismal candle and a previous generation showed up in spirit.

A couple of hours later, we were full. Three baptisms. Eight new members. Kids singing, "You are the light of the world, O people." Bread and Wine. Pancakes. Glitter all over the font, the altar, the carpet. The sweet fragrance of baptismal oil lingering in the air.

I found my colleague alone in the library in his shirt sleeves and vest. Tidying up and beaming, he said, "Anybody would look at this place and know we did church here today."

And I replied, "Pastor, you have glitter all over your face."

Lent, Holy Week, and Easter

L ent and Holy Week likely aren't the way we would choose to go if we were left to work out messy baffling things like life and death on our own. Who would choose the way of the cross as a stopping point along the way to new life?

Lent and Holy Week help us prepare to remember the troubling and transforming way of the cross. And Easter sends us forward to remember, ahead of time, a hope we cannot see and a peace we cannot make for ourselves.

In this season, we will pause by the coffee urn perched on the counter in the church kitchen to remember and give thanks to God in Christ for the gift of simple hospitality. We'll visit a hospital chapel and have a disarming opportunity to witness life and death in close proximity. We'll pause with Jesus outside the open tomb to scrutinize[1] his wounded hands, right in the exact place where his assailants hammered in those brutal nails. Before reaching Easter, we'll eat supper with Jesus just before his crucifixion. And only then, after the crucifixion, will we fast-forward to our own resurrections and the sparkling radiance each of us disciples will share with the crucified and risen Christ.

Fasten your seat belts; here we go.

---

1. According to https://www.etymonline.com, "Perhaps the original notion of the Latin word scrutinize is 'to search among rubbish,' *via scruta* (plural) 'trash, rags, rubbish' ('shreds'); or the original sense might be 'to cut into, scratch.'"

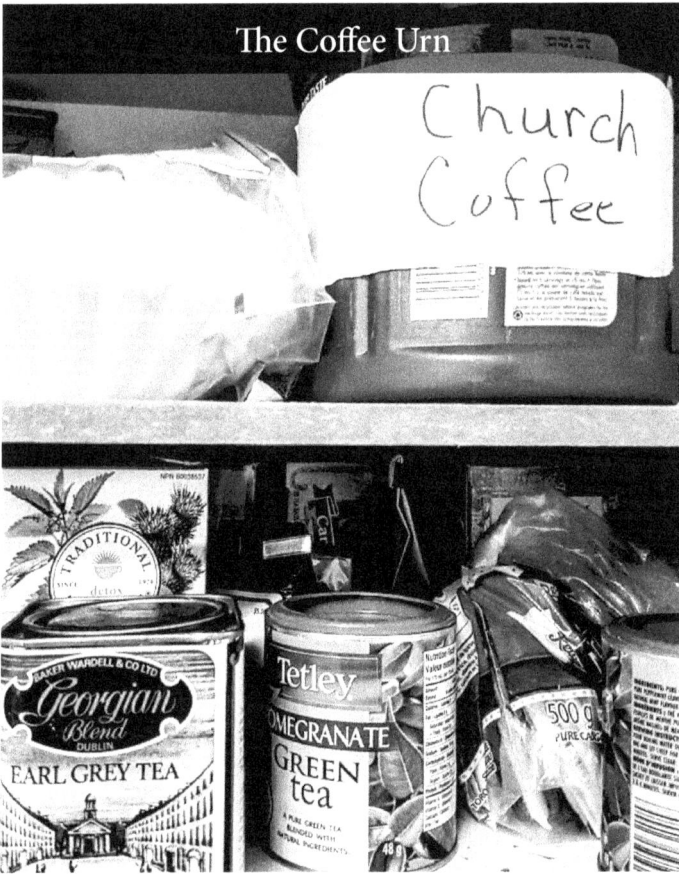

The Coffee Urn

Church Coffee

"Hope locates itself in the premise that we don't know what will happen
and in the spaciousness of uncertainty is room to act."

REBECCA SOLNIT[1]

1. Rebecca Solnit, *Hope in the Dark: Untold Histories, Wild Possibilities.*
(New York: Nation Books, 2004), *xiv.*

O n the Wednesday afternoon before Holy Week, I was upstairs in my study, preparing for our final midweek Lenten service when the phone rang. On the other end of the line was our church Office Manager calling to say that an out-of-town couple had dropped in and asked to talk to a pastor. Because our church was on the main street, folks often dropped in unannounced; daily occasions for mission and ministry kept knocking on what an Office Manager called "the revolving door." As a newly-ordained pastor, it was part of my call to help the congregation see and respond to opportunities for outreach.[2]

So, I went downstairs to meet the couple. The woman appeared strikingly Goth with her raven-black hair, thick dark makeup, and black clothing. The man seemed much younger in blue jeans and sweatshirt. They introduced themselves as husband and wife, saying they were "just passing through."

We spent some time in my study, and what struck me was that they didn't ask for anything. And they were vague about their background. Though I didn't ask many questions, I was increasingly intrigued about who they were and what they were really looking for when they asked to talk with a pastor.

When we ran out of things to say, I was still none the wiser about whatever they were trying to ask or tell me. The conversation seemed to have trickled down to pointlessness. If there *was* a point, I couldn't see it. So after about an hour, I walked downstairs with them to the kitchen where I knew someone was sitting there, quietly waiting.

And there he was, in his usual spot by the percolating coffee urn, perched on a stool after setting up tables and chairs for the Lenten potluck supper later on.

I introduced the mysterious couple and right away this man (I'll call him the host) poured hot coffee for all of us. He wasn't dispensing charity; he was extending hospitality. Soon, the couple were chatting with him, so I disappeared upstairs until it was time

2. Harold Remus tells his version of the origin story of Community Ministry in the book *See You Next Week* with the title "From a Small Seed," 17–18. "The Host" has given his permission to tell this story. His written permission on file.

34

for the meal. Who knows how many others dropped by the kitchen for a cup of coffee and a little chat?

When I returned later, more folks were starting to gather and visit. The serving table was spread with casseroles, salads and desserts. And the mystery couple was still there. Among us. By then, in that open, spontaneous way of his, the host had invited them for supper. As the group had done every other Wednesday, we prayed an old table grace, faithfully answered in every generation: "Come, Lord Jesus, be our guest." And then we served ourselves and settled in to enjoy good food and each other's company.

As people headed into the sanctuary for worship after the meal, the visiting couple smiled and said thank you. Before they headed out the door, one of them said four little words that would leave an indelible mark on our day-to-day parish ministry: "See you next week."

See you next week? Well, um, no. Though I didn't say it aloud, that's what I was thinking. Lent would be over next week, and there would be no mid-week potluck. By the following Wednesday, we'd be in the middle of Holy Week.

Yet, the words, "See you next week" called for a quick decision, a decision that took about ten long seconds and resulted only in a few nods. Following our host's example of a Christ-like response, someone turned to the couple and filled the awkward gap with "Great then! See you next week."

And space opened up.

For one meal at a time, they came back.

Without the slightest idea of what would happen next and who we'd meet, the church at the corner of King and Green began offering free weekly Wednesday night community suppers. Through storms and sunshine and blossoming ecumenical and community partnerships. Through hiring the first of several Community Ministers with help from the wider church. Through changes of church leadership, changes of format, changes of government. Through showing up on the radar of the supportive Public Health Unit and transitioning from potlucks to meals prepared by a Kitchen Coordinator in a licensed kitchen. Through investing in a commercial dishwasher and the donation of a bigger, better, fridge and freezer. The meals continued in global pandemic when they were served in paper bags after the move to form a new, amalgamated congregation with a new name in another location uptown.

The mystery couple had long since moved on, yet week by week the supper community grew in numbers and in simple human warmth. The church building grew busier. People just kept showing up. They invited their friends. Those friends invited *their* friends. There was no withdrawal to a quiet place and prayers for discernment[3]. No feasibility studies. No publicity. No vote. And, no budget. At least in the beginning. We church folks had a lot to learn from the host who prepared a place. He set up tables, brewed a big urn of hot coffee, and poured two cups for an out-of-town couple who'd arrived among us for complicated and mysterious reasons. Hey, maybe the host only *plugged in* the coffee urn. Early in the day, the custodian often filled the urn with water and measured out the coffee, and then someone else like the host plugged the urn in later in the day.

How humbling it can be when we believers pray, "Come, Lord Jesus, be our guest" and then live into a future when Jesus answers our prayer in surprising ways, a future we might not choose for ourselves, a future yet to be received and explored.

Soon the word was out, and other guests showed up—including the Host with a capital "H" who had been there all along. His story includes that odd incident about feeding five thousand tired and hungry people with five loaves and two fish.[4]

How did *that* happen? It was like this. Like the church treasurer who expressed uneasiness with the meal and so many strangers streaming into the church every day yet offered to bake chicken thighs with his special barbecue sauce. Enough for all. He scoured newspaper ads and waited until chicken thighs went on sale at the market across the street. This same man left the church whistling after he delivered armloads of daffodils to the church in the springtime. It must have been like the retired couple who drove

3. Matthew 14:13, Luke 4:22, Luke 15:16, Matthew 14:13. *NRSV.*

4. Matthew 14:13-21, Mark 6:31-44, Luke 9:12-17, John 6:1-14. *NRSV.*

their old Cadillac to the Campbell's Soup factory in a village out in the country to pick up big plastic containers of frozen soup, or the woman who quietly delivered leftover bagels to the church after her shift ended at the coffee shop next door in the hospital lobby. She popped the bagels into the freezer, and disappeared unseen.

It must have been like the young mother and her preschool daughter who spent a morning each week for a season baking and decorating cupcakes in the church kitchen and leaving them out on the counter to share with whoever showed up. Or the church usher who one Wednesday arrived with a beautiful salmon and baked it over fruited rice and disappeared at serving time. Or the many who delivered ripe tomatoes from their gardens during the summer months. None of these folks made a big deal about what they contributed. They came up with their own ideas of how to feed a bunch of hungry people with five loaves and two fish.

Who could ever have imagined that a common coffee urn perched on the counter in an old church kitchen would be the start of such widespread hospitality?

Two cups of steaming coffee.

A little chat.

A potluck supper ready to be shared.

The arrival of enigmatic strangers with unexpressed needs.

And wonder of wonders: the multiplication of much more than loaves and fishes.

Poem: Sanctuary of the Impossible[1]

In a world where we are the ones who are deaf and asking,
And you are the one who is supposed to be listening and answering,
how are you going to work this one out God?
In a world where our friend lives in the cemetery,
and celebrates his birthday every day of the year,
how are you going to get the gifts to the party?
Show us, we say, as we stand here in line
in the sanctuary of the impossible
with everyone who breathes,
doubters and dreamers, exiles and pilgrims,
panhandlers and witches, the young and the restless,
the addicted and lonely, card players and clerics,
the sweet and the scornful, stargazers and savants,
the gardener who sets up the tables,
the woman who lets the children go first,
Santa Claus and the Avon Lady,
the man with the box accordion.
Here in the sanctuary of the impossible,
where our friend lives in a cemetery called Mount Hope
and celebrates his birthday every day of the year.
Behold!

1. Nancy Vernon Kelly, "Sanctuary of the Impossible," was inspired by Psalm 150:6 and was first published in *See You Next Week: An Ecumenical Community Ministry in Downtown Kitchener* (Kitchener: Community Ministry), 71. Reprinted here with permission.

Holy Week

"Death be now but never last."

RAY MAKEEVER[1]

1. "Death Be Never Last," Text and music: Ray Makeever. ©1993, Ray Makeever, admin. Augsburg Fortress. Hymn No. 1030, "All Creation Sings," Minneapolis: Augsburg Fortress, 2020. Retrieved May 8, 2022.

W e formed a little circle in front of the altar in the hospital chapel. Above us, the majestic "Tree of Life" banner[2] soared up to the skylight. It was Holy Week when I went to the hospital on that warm early spring day. Upon learning that several women from our faith community were patients in the same hospital, I had reserved the chapel for us. With the help of hospital porters, we met there to share communion.

Though it was the most somber week in the Church Year, the occasion started out on a surprisingly festive note. Until that morning, the three women hadn't known they were all patients in the same hospital; they giggled like little girls to meet each other there. I was hoping for a cozy, candlelight communion service along with a reunion in the peaceful chapel. Little did we know who was coming to join us!

When we were about half-way through our reading of the story of Jesus' crucifixion, two hospital orderlies in scrubs, as if accompanied by a solemn Good Friday requiem, pushed a gurney with a shrouded body up to the front of the chapel. They were doing their job, accompanying somebody who had just died on one of the units. The death certificate had been signed. The person's possessions were gathered up in plastic bags. If there were any family members or a chaplain at the bedside at the moment of death, they were gone now. It was up to the orderlies to do their part. With matter-of-fact skill and reverence, the two men maneuvered the gurney around us worshippers and opened the door beside the altar.

I stopped reading, mid-sentence, and my open bible dropped into my lap. Whew! We, the living, glanced meaningfully at one another, then lowered our heads. In silence. To make room for someone worth stopping for and making room for. To make room for an eventuality we were powerless to change. To make room for a sacred intrusion.

In a way, the interruption was perfectly timed. We were listening to the story of Jesus' death. But this was no prayerfully planned and rehearsed Good Friday chancel drama. This was a

---

2. Designed by local fabric artist Nancy-Lou Patterson, 1929-2018.

station of the cross for a flesh-and-blood neighbor. Someone with a life story. A beginning and an end you could mark on a calendar. Someone, hopefully, who was dearly loved as we all long to be loved. Someone who took their last breath out.

After the orderlies delivered the shrouded body to the little room beyond the door, they departed empty-handed, their heads lowered, as quietly as they had entered. Their mission complete, they moved on.

When the three elderly ladies in wheelchairs started a spontaneous conversation with each other, I closed the bible. The women were instinctively, curiously, attentive to our close encounter with death. They wondered among themselves while I listened. They needed to wonder out loud, and I did, too.

Was the dead person somebody we knew? How old were they? How did they die? Were they alone or with someone who loved them when they took their last breath? Did they have a chance to say goodbye? Would we be able to turn to the obituary page in tomorrow's local newspaper and recognize a small part of who the person was?

Under the outreached arms of the Tree of Life, we had a disarming opportunity to witness life and death in close proximity where Christ meets us. Silence was our first and most natural response to this mysterious and unnerving intersection of life and death. Then, for the moment, we set aside our other plans to pause and ask each other questions we couldn't answer.

Wounded Hands

"Wounds and wonders are a both/and.
Wounds are an invitation to enter into the raw and real of human life
and then to wait for the wonder."

DALE CARL FREDERICKSON[1]

1. Dale Carl Fredrickson, *on wounds & wonder,* Steubenpress.com © Dale
Carl Fredrickson, 2017 (np).

S unday after Sunday for many years, I sat in the chancel facing the congregation, aware of so much mortal and moral
need. When I glanced to the side over at the south transept, I
saw three colorfuls resurrection banners, a triptych designed by
a local textile artist[2] and quilted with love by the women of two
faith communities.

Two angels appear in the first banner, guarding the cave
where Jesus was buried. A large boulder—previously thought to be
immoveable—stands beside the entrance to the empty tomb.[3] In
the second banner, the three Marys wait at the entrance with jars of
spices.[4] They're filled with grief, yet not immobilized. They stand
ready to anoint the body of their beloved friend and teacher.

As meaningful as these first two banners were, it was the
third banner that called out to me; it had a voice all its own. Jesus
has just stepped into the daylight on the first morning of his new
life. He has just taken his first breath in, after what was supposed
to be his last breath out. Mary Magdalene is with him. Here stands
one human being who was previously dead and is now alive beside
another human being who is gutted with grief.

Something about the hands of the resurrected Jesus[5] beck-
oned me, and my eyes often rested on the place where his wounds
were still visible. It wasn't merely the sightline from where I was
sitting that drew my eyes to those wounds. The Spirit was in the
mix too, giving eyes to see what was most needed. In the presence of our individual and collective needs that third banner was
bearing witness.

Did Jesus still hurt after he rose up from the dead? I didn't see
smooth, healed-over scars. I saw fresh, red, bloody wounds. What
did the quilters talk about with each other the morning they appliquéd those pieces of bright red cloth onto Jesus' hands? Even after

2. Nancy-Lou Patterson (1929-2018). These resurrection banners now
hang in the chapel of Trillium Lutheran Church in Waterloo, Ontario.

3. Mark 16:1-8, Luke 24:1-12. *NRSV.*

4. Mark 16:1-4, Luke 24:1-2. *NRSV.*

5. John 20:17, John 20:27, Mark 16:9. *NRSV.*

the resurrection, Jesus still looked so vulnerable, so human. The wounds on his flesh-and-blood hands weren't appliquéd.

Ever since my first encounter with that banner, the image of the wounded risen Christ has played havoc with my reflection on resurrected life. Mary Magdalene witnessed Jesus' wounds on Easter morning when she met him alive at the door to the open tomb. The following week, at Jesus' gracious invitation, Thomas reached out to touch those same wounds. And there was a mysterious and life-affirming energy flowing from them.

My response to the quilted image of Jesus' hands was to begin a conversation with his wounds. If they could talk, what would they say? All I needed was to look out over the pews and into the faces of choristers up in the chancel and inside myself to feel the gathered weight of all our wounds. Stalking there and beyond the sanctuary were so many complicated wounds in the fabric of our lives—broken relationships, illness, grief, addiction, abuse, poverty, racism, hatred, indifference. Not to mention wars and rumors of war in the wider world. Quiet wounds, and wounds longing to bear witness to the truth of the injustices that caused them.

No matter how exuberant our Alleluias, our wounds are real. Wounds to show, or perhaps to hide. When the risen Christ meets the disciples after being raised from the dead, he reveals a mystery. Wounds are no contradiction in the resurrected life. And the wonder is that God, who isn't the cause of our traumas and wounds, often uses our wounds to offer hope for new life.

Fluffy Bath Towels

*"Jesu, Jesu, fill us with your love, show us how to serve,
the neighbors we have from you."*

TOM COLVIN[1]

1. Tom Colvin, "Jesu, Jesu, Fill us with Your Love" in *Evangelical Lutheran
Worship*. (Minneapolis: Augsburg Fortress, 2006), No. 708.

45

O ne year on Maundy Thursday we decided on *hand*-washing instead of foot-washing so more people could participate. After the first time, the ritual stuck, and hand-washing became the heart of our Maundy Thursday worship. This is a story about almost everybody participating in the enlivening power of up-close, firsthand, tactile participation in a redemptive ritual. Was it a bit uncomfortable? Surely, for some of us it was. Imagine how uncomfortable the first disciples must have been when Jesus got down on his knees and washed their dirty feet. This is a story about a woman who, like Jesus, fearlessly shared an intimate, physical connection with her companion worshippers.

First, we read the story.[2] Not long before Jesus dies, after the last supper he shares with his friends, he takes a towel, gets down on his knees, and washes his disciples' feet. Peter doesn't buy this idea and objects, declaring that *he,* Peter, the rock on whom Jesus promised to build his church, will be the one to wash *Jesus'* feet. But Jesus is a different kind of leader. Not a micromanaging, controlling, organizing, administering kind of leader. Jesus is a *servant* leader with a servant heart who bends down and washes his disciples' feet. More than that, he calls us to do the same.

After reading the story, we *enacted* the story in our own lo-cal way, using the gifts at hand, including each other. Our ritual was simple and communal. Inside our antique wooden font sat a striking modern ceramic bowl.[3] For the handwashing, we used ordinary warm tap water in ceramic pitchers, and fluffy bath towels just like the ones we all used at home to dry off after a shower.

That night, we moved toward the font in pairs, slowly, lov-ingly, warmly, without pretense. Couples who knew each other's hands well. Old friends. Strangers. Parents and small children. Grandparents and grandchildren. At this service, our vulnerabil-ity connected us.

Each year, a few days before Maundy Thursday, a woman phoned one of the pastors. The conversation was predictable. She intended to be the one to dry people's hands. She wasn't offering.

2. John 13:1-17. *NRSV.*

3. Pictured on the book cover.

She was *telling* us she would do it. She planned to come for the afternoon service and would return in the evening. I came to believe she was one of God's best surprises.

This woman didn't go to church; she went to churches. She lived in a small apartment downtown, across the street from the bus terminal, in a repurposed school building. And she was a perceptive theologian who knew the scriptures well and was beyond determined to share her own blunt commentary.

During our Monday morning bible studies on the Gospel reading for the following Sunday, she often arrived late and immediately seemed to fall asleep on an upholstered loveseat in the church parlor. Every so often she'd open her eyes and chime in—POW!—as the rest of us (supposedly awake) sat in a circle sipping Red Rose Tea in mismatched church mugs, puzzling over what we could learn about Jesus.

The woman had a way of making Jesus' message clear:

"Well, didn't Jesus tell us to love our neighbors?"

"I thought he found a way to feed *all* the hungry people."

"Anyway, why *wouldn't* you just forgive your enemies?"

She also loved to dry people's hands. For the Maundy Thursday ritual, it was so obvious she had been called to carry out this labor of love. This was her vocation and her offering: gathering up a soft towel, unfolding it deliberately and lovingly, draping it over her own outstretched hands, and fulfilling her ministry of gently drying the hands of others. She looked each one of us in the eyes and offered as earnest a word of forgiveness as I have ever heard: "Christ sets you free to love and serve."

The Gooseneck Lamp (Easter Vigil)

"There is something about . . . wonder, as in, awe,
as in, I had no idea I would be here now."

ARIANA BROWN[1]

1. Ariana Brown, "For everyone who tried on the slipper before Cinder-ella" in Poem-a-Day. (Academy of American Poets, October 14, 2022). https://poets.org/poem/everyone-who-tried-slipper-cinderella. Retrieved November 28, 2022.

T his is another story about the woman who dried our hands on Maundy Thursdays. She was also one of our most expressive readers. Even now, I can hear her clear, dignified voice coming over the sound system from the lectern, reaching every corner of the sanctuary. This memory is now part of her eternal life. She was on the regular roster of readers, and she also loved to serve as one of many readers at our annual Easter Vigil.

One year, on Holy Saturday, the woman arrived early at church and burst into my study wearing an astonishing gold-sequined bomber jacket. When I was appropriately bedazzled, she leaned in, and said "Pastor Nan, *everyone* has their own radiance." I posted her words on the bulletin board in my study. And considered getting a tattoo.

On that particular Easter Eve, as on all other Easter Eves, the inside of the church was dark except for the newly-lit paschal candle we'd just processed into the church, and the light of the gooseneck reading lamp at the lectern by the big bible. The woman in the astonishing gold-sequined bomber jacket popped up by the lamp; she was the first to read. That's when I started thinking of her as The Sparkler. The story she read went all the way back to the beginning when God called everything good. To the time and place where the sun first shone and the breath of life began.

Our tradition in reading this story was to involve everybody. At the end of each of the seven Creation days, the reader would say, very slowly, "And it was evening, and it was morning" and with hearing those words, the entire congregation, especially the kids, would holler, "The first day." Or "The second day." "The third day." Voices grew louder and louder as the woman told the story all the way up to Day Seven, as the rest of us cheered for God. Or cheered *with* God.

Thumbing through an old book, I discover a note I wrote long ago in the margins. The note was a rhetorical question followed by my answer:

Q: *What is the best there is?*

A: *The Sparkler in her astonishing gold-sequined bomber jacket reading the Creation Story at the Easter Vigil in the near dark church, shining on us with a light we weren't expecting.*

As The Sparkler herself whispered to me, the Creator of everything gives every single one of us our own sparkling radiance to shine in the shadows.

And indeed, it is very good.[2]

2. Paraphrased from Genesis 1:31. NRSV.

Wherever You Go

Wherever you go,
I will follow you.
You know that, don't you?
In voices loud and clear.
In mumbles and whispers.
In shouts and alarming truths.
I will seek you out.
I'll want to be in the choir.
Stay for coffee and share a hot meal.
I'll seek out a kind, listening ear
and a hand to hold on the coldest, darkest days.
I'll invite you into my story
and summon you to the places I pace.
Sometimes,
I'll be transfigured.
Hard to miss.
I'll be wearing my alarming gold-sequined bomber jacket
and proclaiming the good news:
Everyone has their own radiance.
Other times,
I'll be wearing my funeral clothes,
hoping to grab an egg salad sandwich
off a crystal tray.

If need be,
I'll remind you
to unlock the doors of the church
so I can come in.
On and on,
in whispers and shouts,
I will always insist:
Wherever you go,
I will go with you.
Indeed, I am already here.

Pentecost

I confess that I am among the believers whose hearts begin to soar when we arrive at the point in the Apostles' Creed where we affirm "I believe in the Holy Spirit." My voice wants to crescendo on the words, "I believe in the Holy Spirit, the holy catholic church, the communion of saints, the forgiveness of sins, the resurrection of the body, and life everlasting."

Church music professor and author Paul Westermeyer lists the action verbs that the Pentecost hymn, "Spirit of Gentleness" uses to describe the work of the Holy Spirit. In his *Hymnal Companion to Evangelical Worship,* Westermeyer says: "The Holy Spirit is an active partner who blows, stirs, calls, frees, moves, coaxes, creates, awakens, sweeps, stings, goads, speaks, sings, cries, whispers, and breaks all forms of bondage."[1]

The Holy Spirit acts!

Wow!

The Holy Spirit has been creating since the beginning of time, ever since God said, "Let there be light!" The Holy Spirit filled Jesus from the manger, to the cross, and beyond. In baptism, God plants in each one of us that same power to create what hasn't been created yet and redeem all of Creation that still longs to be delivered and set free.

1. Paul Westermeyer, *Hymnal Companion to Evangelical Lutheran Worship.* (Minneapolis: Augsburg Fortress, 2010), 209. In his commentary, Westermeyer quotes these verbs from the hymn "Spirit, Spirit of Gentleness."

The Holy Spirit also empowers us to build bridges and partnerships that form stepping-stones on the path to peace. In the following stories, I invite you to celebrate the gift of peace itself, to recognize the source of peace, and to acknowledge how incredibly vulnerable and in need of nurture this endangered gift can be.

Come along with me to visit a community-created Peace Garden planted in front of a church, hear an invitation to experience the wonder of partnerships, and, perhaps, shed some tears. We will stop at the busy laneway between the church and the neighboring high school, pausing to reflect on the redemptive potential of contested spaces. Then, I'll invite you to join me in East Africa on one day among many when the Holy Spirit was busy building bridges among people with different understandings of God.

The Peace Garden

"Attentiveness is the natural prayer of the soul."

NICOLAS MALEBRANCHE[1]

1. Nicolas Malebranche (1638-1715), *The Search after Truth* (end of Book 6). Public Domain.

T ry to see it! Shovels in the earth to the glory of God. Stepping stones made with the imprint of rhubarb leaves. The stone bench. Creating the Peace Garden was a hands-on act of prayer, embodied in loving attention to detail.

One spring, the Horticulture Department of the neighboring high school designed and planted the garden in front of the church's main King Street entrance, in a spot where everyone who drove by could see it. A place where walkers could stop to rest awhile and reflect.

When Mr. R., the horticulture teacher, noticed the Peace Pole on a knoll near the corner of King and Green Streets, he imagined much more. He could see something that wasn't there yet on that busy corner. He thought the Peace Pole's prominent location would be the perfect place for his students to plan, plant, and tend a garden. The church's property team, most of them had long-ago graduated from the high school, agreed with the plan and were eager to help. I can still see them down on their knees weeding, tending the earth. For some of them, this memory is part of their eternal life.

Mr. R. cared about peace-building in the high school, in our community, and in the world. He also cared about being a good steward of the land. He and his students had planted a vegetable plot and many kinds of fruit trees on school property and shared their harvest with our weekly community suppers.

After envisioning the corner's potential as a peaceful urban oasis, Mr. R. drew up an inspiring landscape design to share with us. Church members immediately connected with the idea of us teaming up with the students to create a Peace Garden.

Not only did Mr. R. put his own vigor and his whole heart into the project, he also rallied a team of students who worked hard alongside him to haul and shovel, sprinkle and sweat their way through the season it took to make our shared garden dream a reality.[2]

2. Landscape design created by Patrick Rittinger, Horticulture Department at Kitchener-Waterloo Vocational and Collegiate Institute (KCI) Re-printed here with his permission.

Design plan of the Peace Garden created by Patrick
Rittinger. St. Mark's Archives, used with permission
of Mr. Rittinger.

When someone suggested we invite the congregation to
donate plants in honor of loved ones, some 20 families and in-
dividuals pored over Mr. R.'s wish-list, resulting in donations
and pledges toward purchasing a Burning Bush, a Chicago Peace
Rose, Catmint, Lily-of-the-Valley, and a Lenten Rose. More and
more pledges arrived, enough to add a Butterfly Bush, Stained
Glass Hostas, Happy Returns Daylilies, Ferns, Honeysuckle Vines,
and Black-Eyed-Susans. To enhance their beauty, a stone bench,
birdbath, flagstones and topsoil appeared. With his horticultural
genius, Mr. R. had chosen the perfect plants to reflect our shared
theme of peace. He headed for the nursery and came back with
his truck filled with plants, topsoil, and mulch. The garden's daily
progress filled many hearts with gratitude and hope.

Finally, after many weeks, we were ready to celebrate the
completion of the project. One sunny late spring afternoon, the
church and high school jointly dedicated the Peace Garden. A
few years before, the congregation had already dedicated the

Peace Pole on Pentecost, a joyful day when we delighted in festive red streamers rippling over our heads as we processed out the front doors of the church. During the Peace Garden's first season, an elder from the nearby Six Nations community at Ohsweken, Ontario led the Land Acknowledgement, blessing this place as the traditional terrain of the Haudenosaunee, Anishnaabe, and Neutral Indigenous peoples.

The Peace Garden was a shared collective labor of love. Not only was it next door to the city's oldest high school, the area's largest hospital was located on the opposite side.[3] Significantly, the church stood between them, all of us neighbors on Holy Ground in the midst of a vibrant community transitioning from its industrial roots to a 21st-century technology hub. During this time, we faced heartbreaking challenges as we witnessed the needs of our increasingly diverse neighbors: chronic poverty, homelessness, isolation and loneliness, addiction, racism, mental health crises, and cutbacks in government assistance. We also faced significant challenges as a congregation: minimal parking, declining numbers, decreasing offerings, an aging membership, an even older building, and differing visions of what it means to "be the church."

The Peace Garden's dedication happened right in the middle of these complex realities. Yet, in a spirit of thanksgiving for the gift of community and our shared longing for peace, we gathered to celebrate a beautiful oasis planted by volunteers, young and old. We gave thanks for the earth below and the sky above. For Peace Roses, Burning Bushes, Lilies and Hostas. And for honeysuckle, poppies, sunflowers, and weeping pine. For neighbors and neighborhoods. For teachers and students. For muscles digging up the sod. For topsoil and mulch. For our busy city. For all who lived and worked there. For community and the joy of being outside together in the sunshine.

3. In his sermon at the opening service of St. Mark's in 1938, founding pastor Rev. Jacob Maurer said, "St. Mark's is situated between an institution of education and an institution of mercy . . . This building is a challenge to you to go forth as a mighty influence in this community." St. Mark's archives, courtesy of Diane Bonfonte.

Finally, we gave thanks for Mother Earth, for the diversity of her inhabitants and their many languages, some engraved on the Peace Pole: Cayuga (one of Canada's first written indigenous languages), English, German, Hebrew, Arabic, American Sign Language, Spanish, and Amharic (spoken by the Ethiopian and Eritrean congregation that also made its home at the church.).

The Peace Pole publicly proclaimed "May peace prevail on earth" in these eight languages, among the many spoken by (and signed by) people at the church, the high school and the hospital—a daily prayer for so many of us in response to unceasing conflicts around the globe.

May peace prevail on Earth. A prayer still laden with hope and uncertainty as I write this during the ongoing horrors and devastation of Russia's invasion of Ukraine that started in 2022 and the renewed threat of the use of nuclear weapons. And also now, during the relentless news cycle reporting the bloodshed and human cost of war to both sides in Israel and Palestine since October 2023.

Years ago, on that sun-washed noontime, we dedicated this special garden, and ourselves, to peace. We longed for peace by making peace. After the service the congregation invited the high school students and teachers to a "Peace of Pizza Garden Party," a rare and welcome chance to build more bridges as we enjoyed the results of our shared work and each other's company.

Sadly, the Peace Garden, like our vision of peace itself, proved to be an endangered species. About a decade later, when the regional government began building a long-awaited light rail transit system along King Street, the masterplan included slicing off the frontage of the land. This plan meant a goodbye, without reprieve, to what had become a flourishing Peace Garden in the center of our city. It was heart-breaking to see the iconic Peace Pole cut down and the garden demolished.

Amid the Peace Garden's tragic demise, something quietly beautiful and redemptive also happened. Another prayer, from another attentive heart. When a church staff member received warning that the garden would soon be excavated out of existence, she took that brief window of opportunity to dig up as many of the dedicated plants as possible and lovingly relocate them, some temporarily in her own garden. Her merciful act was inspired by a member of the quilting group she attended at our partner church around the corner. There, a fellow quilter revealed that she regularly rescued perennial plants from the gardens of buildings being torn down. Thanks to one gardener's inspiration and another's last-minute efforts, many healthy Peace Garden plants were no longer doomed. They're thriving!

The quest for peace on both a local and international scale is an unfinished mission. Our pursuit of such a vulnerable, valuable gift calls out to us to tend and nurture signs of peace wherever they spring up, even tentatively. And, when things go wrong, to look for and find another way and to keep believing that the pulse of the Gospel transcends the harsh edges that threaten to tear us apart.

Here, Now

We are here now,
still summoned
to build bridges.

The Laneway

"There is no them. There is only us."

LUIS ALBERTO URREA[1]

1. Krista Tippett, host, "Borders are Liminal Spaces." On Being (National Public Radio podcast interview with Luis Alberto Urrea), July 12, 2018. https://onbeing.org/programs/luis-alberto-urrea-borders-are-liminal-spaces/.

I am as loyal to the high school beside the church as I am to the far-away school I graduated from. One of my daughters and both grandchildren graduated from KCI, which only deepened the roots of my connection as a pastor of the church next door.

Every September, the high school's principal would invite the church to greet the student body at their first-day-of-school assembly. Also among the guests were the grocery store manager from across the street, a member of the regional police services, and a representative from the hospital next door, all folks the students were likely to encounter throughout their high school careers. The occasion allowed us to reintroduce ourselves as neighbors and continue to build a welcoming bridge between KCI and its surrounding urban community. And, the Community Ministry always invited the students to enjoy breakfast in the Parish Hall every weekday morning and drop in any time they wanted to chat.

Rain or shine, pastors arriving at church in the morning were often greeted by name by both students and teachers. The Office Manager was thankful for their acts of kindness, like the time one stormy winter day when a student held the church door open after she dropped her glasses in the snow.

Another incident was not as benign. In fact, it was downright offensive. As I exited a taxi one bitter winter morning, a student became visibly irritated by us taking up space in the laneway. Yelling obscenities, he scowled and flicked a cigarette butt at us. The epithet smarted. I shooed away its negative energy and moved on.

Yet a good neighbor who either witnessed or heard about the incident decided to call the school. Maybe it was the taxi driver. Maybe the church Office Manager, the Community Minister, or the Music Director. Maybe it was another student or a teacher. I never found out.

A few days later, a hand-delivered letter arrived at the church from a member of the high school's Student Council.

Dear Pastor Nancy:

On Tuesday, February 27, the students of KCI heard over the morning announcements that one of us acted very inappropriately to the taxi driver and you. On behalf of the other 1,426 students at KCI, we express our most sincere apologies.

We would like you to know that we respect and appreciate what you do for our school and community. We would like you to know that the issue is being taken care of and that it disturbs us as much as it must have disturbed you. Please don't allow the actions of one affect how you view KCI as a whole. We offer our most sincere apologies.

"Most sincere apologies." I took them to heart and began wondering what kind of day the offender was having when the insulting gesture and slurs happened. What was going on at home? What kind of support did the student have and need? This incident and the apology became part of why I felt a growing closeness to the entire high school community and the day-to-day concerns of the students and staff.

Our young neighbors surprised and humbled the church by acting to repair the bridge that had been damaged but not broken. They had planted a sapling behind the church the year before—a Siberian crab apple. At the time of the distressing incident, the tree was still small and fragile; not long after, each spring it was covered in beautiful pink and white blossoms above a small plaque that says, "Celebrating Community."

Congregation members, students, hospital visitors and community groups like AA shared the back laneway near the crab apple tree to access the church, the high school, the arena, the hospital, and other nearby buildings and parking lots. Some students gathered there during their breaks to smoke and chat. At least once, a colleague sat out on the big bench-like boulders on the laneway to prepare a couple for their wedding!

Simply put, the laneway behind the church was contested, and often congested, space. It was also a space with abundant potential for the Holy Spirit to bring diverse people together. As members of the same wider community, we sometimes got in one another's way, physically and mentally. Yet the laneway was also an amazing place to make connections. A place to offer a smile or a nod. A place to offer an apology. Holy space. A space set apart to build bridges.

In an answering letter to the high school students, I accepted their apology on behalf of myself and the taxi driver, forgiving the student who was responsible, even though I would never know their name. I also lamented that we "church people" didn't always stop to smile and greet students and thanked the high school for teaching the church something about forgiveness and mending damaged bridges.

Contested and congested spaces, rough spots in hearts, in communities and in the world are places for bridges, built, broken and mended. Places for truth and reconciliation. Building bridges when things go wrong is the work of the Holy Spirit.

Across the Distance

*"For earth had attained to heaven, and
there was no more near nor far."*

ROBERT BROWNING[1]

1. Robert Browning, "Abt Vogler." Public Domain.

A s I look at Google Maps, a surprisingly bleak message appears on the computer screen: "Can't find a way there!" With an exclamation point. Almost like saying, "You can't get there from here. Don't even try."

And yet . . .between two continents, in places 11,975 kilometres apart, I witnessed the building of a bridge. The Holy Spirit we celebrate on Pentecost specializes in finding ways to accomplish goodness and mercy that often seem impossible. The Holy Spirit is the part of God who empowers us to build bridges.

Timing in all stories is important. And historically, the timing of *this* story is especially vital. It happened about a year before 9/11—a year before September 11, 2001 when hijacked planes flew into New York's World Trade Center, the Pentagon, and a rural field near Shanksville, Pennsylvania. The resulting outrage and retribution revealed the deep-seated Islamophobia that already existed across North America. When I traveled to Africa to participate in an eye-opening Lutheran World Federation Muslim-Christian Dialogue in Dar es Salaam, Tanzania, no one could imagine something as horrific as what happened on September 11, 2001. Neither could I have imagined the story I'm about to tell.

Before the dialogue, I spent a week with congregations and people living in a refugee camp in northern Tanzania. Before becoming a pastor, my background was working with congregations to protect, advocate for, and accompany refugees during the process of resettlement. I welcomed the invitation to visit a refugee camp in the far north near Tanzania's border with Burundi. At the time, the United Nations and the Lutheran World Federation were teaming up to help people flee to safety within Tanzania across a border I could see in the distance from a UN checkpoint. This visit brought me close enough to look into a pregnant mother's eyes, minutes after she crossed that border with her many children, to be identified, screened, vaccinated, given a plot of land, and receive a plastic sheet to begin building a new home with sticks and mud. How would this mother have told her family's story in her own voice beyond my limited, meagre impressions and assumptions? Not to mention the language barrier.

I can't remember any time in my long life when I have borne the weight of white privilege as a North American woman more profoundly than I did in that brief, haunting moment. My heart was breaking, knowing that I would soon be leaving for home in Canada while the woman and her family would be staying, perhaps for years, perhaps forever, putting down roots in foreign soil; in soil just across the border from their own soil. In the same red soil.

The next day, my hosts arranged a visit to a prenatal clinic in a refugee camp where a lively group of pregnant women was seated in a circle and giving each other support. They opened their circle to welcome me, and as one woman burst into jubilant song, the others began to sing with her. I hoped the newly-arrived mother I'd met at the border the day before would soon be in their midst, drumming, dancing and singing, and, at just the right time, she would give birth to a healthy baby who would be free from war, upheaval, and lack of basic necessities.

A group of Christian pastors and Muslim imams who worked in the camp welcomed me into a gathering that was already in progress in an open space within the camp enclosure. They were laughing together, clearly enjoying shared camaraderie. Despite the language barrier, I could sense that they knew each other well and had formed bonds of trust. I had never heard of Muslim and Christian faith leaders meeting together, much less having fun!

The vast distance between what I knew then about Christians and Muslims in North America and what I experienced with people in Tanzania revealed possibilities I'd never before considered. Someone took a picture of us lined up in a posed group. Twenty or so East African men from two distinct faith groups, a handful of church workers and me, a white female pastor, a foreign guest who was skeptical that any good could come from a one-day visit. By then, I was overwhelmed after taking a UN helicopter and travelling on bumpy red dirt roads from one place to another, still processing the mixed feelings I experienced when meeting the eyes of a weary mother moments after she reached safety from a war zone. The warm welcome from the diverse faith leaders revived me, body and soul.

After a round of formal greetings and informal presentations, my hosts asked if I had any questions. I responded: "What do you want me to tell my church when I return home to Canada?"

The imams and pastors grew animated. As if with one voice, they told me how hard it was not having access to their scriptures, Bibles and Qur'ans. They asked if the church could locate both holy books for them. Bibles *and* Qur'ans. An utterly unanticipated and unthinkable request.

"Sure," I chirped quickly, not wanting to dissolve the solidarity I was beginning to feel. I promised to take their request home, despite a growing internal doubt about whether any church on earth would actually provide Qur'ans.

Some weeks later, back in Canada, I shared my Tanzanian experiences with an adult Sunday School group. Among my slides was the picture of the East African Muslim and Christian faith leaders, and me. I told the group about the warm welcome and unexpected inter-faith camaraderie I'd experienced for the first time. Then, I boldly dropped that startling request from the imams and pastors for Bibles *and* Qur'ans.

One no-nonsense woman took the pastors' and imam's request to heart. She immediately spoke up, committing to find the means to provide both the Bibles and Qur'ans in the appropriate languages. This proved to be a much bigger pledge than I'd originally made; fulfilling it would take her and other volunteers close to two years, though it took only about a week to fundraise several hundred dollars. Coins from Sunday School children. Bills and cheques from adults. We were beginning to find a little bit of an answer to a heavyweight "How?" question posed in the introductory package for the inter-faith dialogue: "How are we as Christians and Muslims trying to diffuse the tensions between us?"

Ironically, acquiring Qur'ans turned out to be easier than acquiring Bibles. Something we learned is that the original language of the Qur'an is Arabic, which is still universally used in Muslim worship (Qur'an translations are used only for study or personal meditation).

The woman who spearheaded our quest for scriptures was much like the Syrophoenician woman[2] and other passionate, spirited, gutsy New Testament women who pestered Jesus for healing and had their perseverance rewarded. About two years later, the congregation received word that crates of Arabic Qur'ans and Bibles in the Kirundi language had arrived at last from Canada at that faraway refugee camp in Tanzania.

How inadequate Google Maps is when it comes to deeper questions about the route to peace and how to find a way to reach the intersection of near and far!

2. Mark 7:24-30, *NRSV*.

The Variety Store around the Corner

"What we need are stories that open up the possibility of relationships where there are currently none."

PÁDRAIG Ó TUAMA[1]

---

1. Pádraig Ó Tuama, "Imagining Peace," TEDx talk, October 18, 2016. https://www.youtube.com/watch?v=lJfBYz6tab8. Retrieved August 16, 2022.

On September 12, 2001, while walking back to church after a meeting where leaders of various local faith community leaders had discussed the horrors of the day before, I stopped at a variety store to buy a bottle of orange juice. The store was around the corner from St. Mark's on one side, and next door to Calvary Memorial United Church on the other side. A Muslim family owned the store.

When I went to pay for my bottle of juice, one of the owners was at the cash register, anxiously telling another customer about something that happened to him the day before, the day which would forever be infamously remembered as 9/11. That same day—just hours after two planes flew into New York's World Trade Center twin towers, another struck the Pentagon in Arlington, Virginia and a fourth crashed in a field near Shanksville, Pennsylvania—someone had stormed into the variety store yelling, "Get out of our country!" Yet our neighbor and his family were in *their* chosen country, living their lives in their chosen community, running their store. And they were afraid.

When I shared this story, the Chair of our Community Ministry Committee suggested writing a letter of support to the store owner and his family. By the time of our next meeting, he had drafted a letter and read it to the rest of us out loud. Without question, we people of faith from two neighborhood churches signed the letter. That same dark and rainy September evening, we walked to the variety store to deliver the letter in person.

Slowly and carefully, the owner read these words of support:

September 19, 2001

Dear Friends:

We are members of the Community Ministry Committee at St. Mark's Lutheran Church at the corner of Green and King Street, next to the high school, and of Calvary Memorial United Church next to you on Park Street.

> *As your neighbors, we want to extend our support of you in this critical time. We appreciate the diversity of Canadian society and culture and the many gifts that persons of diverse backgrounds contribute to our country. We appreciate having you and your store in this neighborhood. You are contributing significantly to the well-being of this neighborhood.*
>
> *There is likely no religion and no people that lack hurtful people and hurtful acts. This is certainly true of our religion, Christianity, and the country, Canada, where we live. We pray and hope that we may all learn—together— to put away hate and terror, to grow in love for one another and to seek the justice that rights the wrongs of individuals and of society and protects the weakest and the marginalized in society, both here and around the world.*
>
> *We greet you with the words we extend to one another in our worship services—God's peace be with you.*

Our neighbor, clearly moved by this unexpected expression of support, thanked us and invited our group to stay a while. He treated us to coffee and hot chocolate as we laughed together and appreciated being inside out of the rain.

A number of months later it was Good Friday, the day when we made an annual neighborhood pilgrimage carrying a big wooden cross and stopping at points along the way, such as a large insurance company that provided free office space and was a good corporate citizen, the Regional Social Services building, and an Out of the Cold site.

Our first stop was the corner variety store. The minister of our partner church, Calvary Memorial, repeated the story of what had happened to our Muslim friend the day after 9/11. And he reminded us about what had happened to so many others on that horrific day, when the entire world seemed paralyzed in shock. Then he asked the variety store owner if he'd like to add any words. We waited reverently in the parking lot, a couple of us carrying the heavy cross.

Our neighbor nodded and thanked us for stopping by. Then, as we parted, he extended God's power and imagination to reach out in peace across the borders, barriers and insults that are determined to keep us divided.

He simply said, "Peace be with you."[2] The place where new life begins.

2. John 20:19, John 20:20-22, John 20:26-28. *NRSV.*

Ordinary Time(s)

Ordinary Time, also called the Time after Pentecost, is a time to celebrate the Holy Spirit's power to enlarge, to widen, to broaden and to deepen. We watch the fruits of the Spirit ripening in our seasonal scripture readings. We listen to and reflect on stories about the fruits we ourselves and others are bearing as we grow and change and, inevitably, make messes and become weary. Of course, ordinary time isn't just a season of the Church Year. Ordinary time is *all* time, pregnant with meaning and potential. With grief and moving on. With messiness and with wonder. With broken pots and an unending stream of life-giving water. For now, I invite you to join me in taking the liberty of calling this season Ordinary Time(s).

In the following stories, the power of the Holy Spirit acts in down-to-earth, mortal and moral ways in this fractured, fearful and anxious world where everyone everywhere is created in the image of God. In little everyday, everywhere children and adults, in deepest sadness, amidst overflowing joy, in emerging, baffling questions, and in topsy-turvy wonder, in ordinary times, the Holy Spirit is creating and redeeming still.

Child by Child

"Each one of us is a God-carrier."

ARCHBISHOP DESMOND TUTU[1]

1. Krista Tippett, host, interview with Archbishop Desmond Tutu. Podcast "On Being." National Public Radio, 2010. https://onbeing.org/programs/remembering-desmond-tutu/.

J esus' life embodies the possibility of living change through one person at a time, often one improbable person. In Jesus' upside-down wisdom, people without status or power are gathered at the center of his circle.[2] This is a story about the transformative power of a baby.

When the retired carpenter could no longer come to Sunday morning worship, his Home Communion Minister celebrated the sacrament with him about once a month. A few times a year, I was also able to commune with him. On those occasions, he'd sit in an easy chair by the back window overlooking his patio. Often, he reminisced about his early years in Germany before World War II.

He didn't talk much about the war years, however. The time he spent as a prisoner in a concentration camp. The time when he experienced the power of willful hate, the intentional plan to eliminate an entire people, and to sap the lifeblood of many others. Memories of that deadly power drained all beauty from the old man's face.

One story that restored his serenity was about witnessing a wholly different kind of power. A deep peace settled on his features as he told me about one special afternoon before the war. He was still an awkward teenager, still in his home village. From time to time, he'd drop in on his schoolteacher for a visit. That afternoon seemed no different from the others. He let himself in the front door as he'd done many times before and headed to the kitchen looking for his teacher.

There, at the kitchen table by the window, he saw his teacher's wife breastfeeding the couple's newborn baby. He had never before seen a mother breastfeed her child. As a much older man, his face came alive as he remembered his sense of wonder and awe; he sighed, his eyes brimming with tears.

He recalled the wild stirring and how speechless and bashful he felt. As a teenager, he knew he was experiencing the infinite power of love. A good and merciful power. A disarming power. As

2. Matthew 19:14. *NRSV.*

a teenager, he had no words to describe what he saw, or to express how he felt.

Leaning against the doorframe, he witnessed the power that can transform the world, one defenseless human being at a time. By the time he told this story, he was a grandfather or perhaps even a great-grandfather, when at last he found the words to describe what he knew. That day so long ago, he knew he was standing on holy ground. Standing in the presence of a power that came straight from God.

Though the old carpenter was blind by the time he told me this story, it seemed he could still see the memory of it through the eyes of his heart. He told many other stories over the years, and none came close to expressing the reverence and awe he felt the afternoon he slipped into his teacher's house and witnessed the wonder of a mother sitting at the kitchen table breastfeeding her baby, nourishing new life.

How like Jesus to welcome the child in all of us to climb up into his wide-open arms where all of us are cherished. Where all of us are fed. Just the thought of it made the old man young.

The Baptismal Font

"Even a fleeting moment of grace can carry us a long way, giving us enough, just enough, to keep going."

THE RIGHT REVEREND MARIANN EDGAR BUDDE
BISHOP, EPISCOPAL DIOCESE OF WASHINGTON[1]

1. Sermon, Washington National Cathedral, August 29, 2021. https://cathedral.org/sermons/sermon-the-right-rev-mariann-edgar-budde-19/. Retrieved October 19, 2021.

From where I sat in the chancel, I could see the little child slowly and deliberately advancing his two brightly colored plastic Brontosaurus friends up the base of the baptismal font. As his beloved creatures moved upward, the boy sang a little song he made up to celebrate his baby sister's baptism. "Getting wet. Today we're getting wet. We're getting wet!"

And—kerplunk! With a dramatic splash, the plastic dinosaurs dove into the water for a swim. Full immersion baptism! Right in a Lutheran church!

One Sunday morning, this same extroverted child yelled out, "Hey Mom, you did it!" after listening to his mother sing a heartwarming soprano solo.

In the middle of another service, a child started tugging on the ends of my liturgical stole. We were at the baptismal font that morning, too, having just confessed our faith in the ancient words of the Apostles' Creed: "I believe in the resurrection of the body and the life everlasting."

On hearing these words, a light went on in the child's five-year-old brain. Words that moments before were reserved for adults no longer went over his young head. He was wide awake! And so innocent and unselfconscious. So sincere. He looked up at me and blurted out, "Were you just talking about my Pappy?" Suddenly, it was as though we were the only two people in the crowded sanctuary.

The time was right. The place was right. The words were right. And the child's heart was like good soil, devoid of thorns, rocks and weeds. His beloved grandfather had just died after a long illness. The little boy had attended the funeral and his heart was wide open to having a spontaneous little chat with an adult about big things that were weighing on his mind—big things like life, death, and resurrection. He was wide open; the way we adults are sometimes wide open when we're grieving.

"Talking about your Pappy?" I answered, deciding the Prayers of the People could wait. "Yes! *Of course,* we're talking about your Pappy. Whenever we say, 'I believe in the resurrection of the body and the life everlasting,' we're talking about your Pappy, and my Pappy, and everybody else who has died."

And for just a moment, no interference or static got in the way. The congregation was still. Adult words like *Creator*, *conceived*, and *crucified* gave way to words anybody can understand: "Were you just talking about my Pappy?" The rocks, thorns, and dryness were dismissed.[2] It was a good soil moment. The life-giving Word of God had gently fallen on that little boy's soil, and when that moment came, it came filled with childlike wonder.

2. Matthew 13:1-23, Mark 4:1-20, Luke 8:4-15. *NRSV.*

That One's Cracked!!

STEPHEN MINISTRY

"This whole thing . . . cracked you open
to everybody's pain and not just your own."

KATE BOWLER[1]

1. Krista Tippett, host, "The Future of Hope." On Being. (National Public Radio podcast conversation between Kate Bowler and Wajahat Ali about their experiences with cancer), September 18, 2021, retrieved December 4, 2022. https://onbeing.org/programs/kate-bowler-and-wajahat-ali-the-future-of-hope/.

During the children's time one Sunday morning, the kids and I walked over to the north transept, where vivid blue stained-glass windows shine with vines and colorful orbs that look like ripe fruit. There, hanging on the wall next to a table with bags of oatmeal, tins of tuna and jars of peanut butter for the Food Bank, hung the banner celebrating Stephen Ministry.

By then, many in the church had embraced Stephen Ministry as a way of life that calls, trains, and supervises laypeople to give one-to-one loving care to others in time of need. Stephen Ministry multiplies the fruits of the spirit in faith communities: goodness and mercy expressed in "love, joy, peace, patience, kindness, generosity, faithfulness, gentleness, and self-control."[2]

On the tenth anniversary of our Stephen Ministry, I decided to introduce the children to the theme of caregiving by showing them the banner. As we approached it, the kids, as usual, were way out ahead of me, and I was bringing up the rear. Turned out there was no need to prepare the children by describing what I saw,[3] the silhouettes of two stick figures standing side by side, intersected by a cross. One of the stick people appears to be whole. The other has an obvious, zig zag lightning-bolt line down the middle.

Before I had a chance to ask the children what *they* saw, one of the younger boys pointed up at the obviously broken, hurting, human body on the banner. He couldn't help himself. "That one's cracked!!" he yelled. That boy needed no mic! People in the back pews and up in the balcony could hear him.

Time stopped then, in the presence of God's people of all ages and so many clamoring needs. Time stopped to attend to the clear voice of one little boy with wide-open eyes, whose innocence and openness I envied. "That one's cracked!!" is all I remember. With deep wisdom, a little child gave us words to describe how broken

2. Galatians 5:22. *NRSV.*

3. The Stephen Ministry organization describes the imagery this way: "The Stephen Ministry logo represents a care receiver's journey from brokenness toward wholeness through the cross of Jesus. In this way, it illustrates 'Christ caring for people through people.'" Stephen Ministry Leader Helen Weber created the banner. For more about Stephen Ministry see https://www.stephen-ministries.org/default.cfm. Retrieved May 25, 2022.

we can be. Though brokenness can be painful to admit, one of the things that unites us is that together we belong to the communion of the cracked. We are all vulnerable,[4] and we are not alone. Sometimes raw, sometimes scabbed over, our cracks are part of what prepares us to reach out and care for others in their need.

Compassionate down-to-earth, flesh-and-blood companionship can become, for us, communion beyond the bread and wine on the bridge between brokenness and wholeness.

4. The root of the English word *vulnerable* is the Latin word *vulnerare,* wound. https://www.etymonline.com/word/vulnerable. Retrieved May 25, 2022.

Each Perfect Gift

*"For each perfect gift of thine . . . Christ, our God
to thee we raise this our sacrifice of praise."*

FOLLIOTT S. PIERPOINT[1]

1. Pierpoint, Folliott S. Anglican educator and poet (1835-1917). "For the
Beauty of the Earth." Public Domain. Text of No. 879 in *Evangelical Lutheran
Worship,* Minneapolis: Augsburg Fortress, 2006.

*D*ear G:[2]

Because there is something I don't want you to forget, I decided to write it down. I doubt I'll ever forget, but you might. You'll grow up and have your eyes on bigger and better tower cranes and construction sites, steam shovels and dump trucks. And in the middle of all that, here's something I hope you'll remember.

You're a big boy now. Ten years old. "Double digits," you announced yesterday, and that's very special. Something else very special happened yesterday. At the Children's Time, I called the kids forward like I always do. You and your little brother and all the other kids ran up to the front of the church and sat cross-legged on the floor. You were front and center when I asked you and the other kids what you're afraid of. I was holding a night light in my hands—that's because the lessons from the Bible were scary that day—all about earthquakes and hunger, dreadful things like problems between parents, brothers, sisters, families and friends. How could we begin to talk about any of that?

So, I decided to ask you a question.

"What are you scared of?"

You were waving your hand wildly and were the first to answer. "Because of my autism I'm afraid of the dark," you said, straight from your heart, the very best gift, the gift of yourself,

"Yes," I said. Something was reaching into my soul, stirring my soul. "Sometimes I'm scared of the dark, too," I said, and right about then your little brother started waving his hand up in the air to catch my attention.

"I'm scared of the hyenas on my wall," he said.

"Whew," I answered. "That'll do it every time. Hyenas on your wall."

I'm so proud of your brother for speaking out in front of the whole congregation, telling us about his problem with hyenas. That's got to take a lot of guts! Maybe there's someone else in the congregation who has a problem with hyenas. They must have felt

---

2. G. is an adult now and re-read this letter before he gave his permission to share it. His brother gave his permission, too.

pretty good just to know they're not alone. Somebody else is afraid of hyenas, too.

After you two guys took the lead, the answers started tumbling out from your friends.

Scared of nightmares.

Scared of monsters.

Scared of getting lost.

Scared in the hospital.

I barely got around to talking about how Jesus is the light of the world, shining in the middle of all our scary times because soon it was time to pray and send you back to your seats.

Only you didn't go back to your seat. After I placed the night light on the altar, I slipped into a pew in front of the pulpit to listen to the preacher. You slipped into the front pew next to me and just sat there as though you were deep in thought. Part way through the sermon you leaned over and whispered to me, "Are you going to give out the bread and wine today?"

"Yes," I whispered back, happy you know communion follows the sermon and also trying not to make a big deal of it so you wouldn't get the idea I wanted to have a little chat during the sermon. "No communion now. A little later."

For a little while longer you didn't say anything else until finally something or someone prompted you to lean over again and say, "I'm going to help."

I must have looked surprised because you repeated yourself very slowly and a little bit more loudly with emphasis just to make sure I understood. "I'm going to help; I'm going to give out the bread."

Pretty soon you were up on your feet, up the aisle, over to the sanitizing gel, right during the sermon, washing your hands, getting ready to serve communion. You were serious and more than ready to get going with communion. And I was pretty sure, with all of us in God's hands, everything was going to be all right.

Fast forward to communion, and there you were standing behind the altar beside me. How tall you must have looked, you just getting into double digits and already half a head taller than I am! When I washed my hands, you washed yours a second time. And right about then everything slowed down as we sang:

"For each perfect gift of thine,

Peace on earth and joy in heaven.

For Thyself, best gift divine

To our world so freely giv-n."

For each perfect gift! The gift of yourself! Freely given! When the time came, I handed you the plate of bread. You were alert, and true to your word, you were completely ready to serve. Gently, I steered you over to where I usually stand to serve the bread, thinking I would stand behind you and say the words while you fed God's people. After that, you just took over.

You weren't shadowing me; I was shadowing YOU! It was as though you'd been serving communion forever! You're great at knowing things by heart; you've always been great at knowing things by heart! Songs and poems and prayers, and you even know the words we say at communion.

One by one, as the people came forward, you said those words all by yourself: "This is the body of Christ, given for you."

I peeked out from behind you to see the glow on people's faces. When they approached you, they looked so hungry and tenderhearted and thankful—and so surprised by the grace of it all. Keep it up. That's what I want to say to you. God has a special purpose for you and for your little brother and for all of us.

Thank you for giving us the perfect gift of yourself yesterday, so freely given, your truth, the very best gift of all.

Love,

Pastor Nancy

Wanted:

Companions
safe and slow
to walk beside us on this old road
that's being torn up
to make way
for the new.

Neighbors
who tune in
to the wavelength
of our hidden
courage.

Fellow travellers
who delight in the broken treasures
we unearth at excavation sites:
a vintage walking cane,
a pocketful of mud-caked rocks,
a splinter from the old road.

Friends
who help us create something new
with these, our treasures,
and our fears.

Circles
that open up
just to see us coming
and settle it once and for all:
"Surely God
is in this place and
we didn't know it."
Surely.

For the one who chose Genesis 28:16
as their confirmation verse

Sign Language

"[Jesus] . . . proclaimed the absolute dignity of every human person who came into his presence."

DR. JOHN PAWLIKOWSKI[1]

1. Dr. John Pawlikowski, "Interpreting the Passion Narratives without Blaming 'the Jews.'" https://youtu.be/-woUhw_xPbk. Retrieved June 2, 2022.

Ordinarily, all who came through the door on a Wednesday night were welcome to fill an empty plate and sit down at the table. No reservations. No questions asked. No cost. From Day One, when a couple of travelers first said "See you next week," these meals were wellsprings of wonder. This is a story about one of many times when wonder was pressed down, and overflowing.

There was one night when the time was ordinary and the place was ordinary, and the ordinary diners enjoyed a meal that was anything but ordinary: a scrumptious spread of pork schnitzel, fries, garden salad, and for dessert a choice of Black Forest or strawberry cheesecake. Or a sliver of each, as long as there was enough.[2]

Here's the backstory only a few knew, for the staff was sworn to secrecy.

A young professional who didn't believe in formal church membership, but hung around St. Mark's anyway, decided to use his income tax return to provide a professionally catered banquet for everyone who showed up. Most of those who ate together on Wednesday nights lived on the margins, economically and socially. Many faced multiple challenges, often due to stereotypes and stigmas that set them apart. The young man with a tax return to give away worked with the Community Minister to pull off a grand surprise for each person who came through the door.

On the night of the feast, each diner—no matter what names we were called during the day, who had our backs (or didn't), whose crumbs we'd been eating just to get by, or our rung on the socio-economic ladder—we all sat down together. We dined at long tables covered with fine linen cloths. Gracious waiters in formal white jackets served an elegant haute cuisine menu prepared by a chef in starched white apron and hat.

The extravagant meal generated many surprised yet grateful squeals and laughter, followed by an enthusiastic round of applause that lifted all the evening's table talk to a prayer of thanksgiving.

Of course, the young man had to insist that the staff keep the glorious banquet a secret right up until the reveal. What would we

---

2. Isaiah 19:6-9, Revelation 19:6-9, Revelation 21:4. *NRSV.*

93

have done if word got out about free schnitzel with all the trimmings, and the whole community showed up? Yet this is a glimpse of the wondrous new life we are all created to share together.

That evening, the unexpected feast—and indeed all our Wednesday Night Suppers—were like sign language pointing us to give thanks to God, who in goodness and mercy is restoring all of us, all God's children, back to the same table where we belong. To where we are all satisfied. To where we are all fed. To where we are all loved, appreciated, wanted, and needed.

What delight rises up at the intersection of our various hungers and unexpected, open-hearted acts of kindness like that meal!

Signage

all life is pointing
colors,
patterns,
vanishing ink
visitations
realizations
conversations
catastrophes
serendipities
synchronicities
all life,
even the wreckage,
is kindling
for goosebumps
and sighs
and all life is signing
pay attention
pass the word

Something Like Roses

"Even when the agenda is bread, what spills over is roses."

REBECCA SOLNIT[1]

1. Rebecca Solnit, *Orwell's Roses.* New York: Viking, 96

For a season, an artist seeking a new beginning hung around St. Mark's and came to our weekly church hall suppers. Like all of us who were on our way to somewhere else—whether we knew it at the time or not—the artist briefly meshed with our community life and then moved on.[2]

Before doing so, she set something beautiful in motion. She persuaded the nearby flower shop called "Mostly Roses" to set aside their leftovers every Wednesday afternoon to dress up our supper tables. Suddenly there was such an abundance of fresh roses! Roses in full bloom, destined for the compost heap. Now, roses redeemed. Lively roses in red, pink, orange and yellow. Expensive *carpe diem* roses on the edge of their "best before" date.

When the artist moved away, another woman carried on her ministry of extravagance, gleaning even more roses from the florist—enough roses every Wednesday to arrange many lavish bouquets to brighten the Parish Hall, church parlor, choir room, offices, and wherever else she saw the need for beauty. She anointed the entire building so that everyone who entered enjoyed an extravagance of roses.

Thanksgiving was the reason. And these women's expressions of thanksgiving were a work of art. There would never have been funds in the Community Ministry's modest budget for anything so extravagant, yet those surprise roses filled an important place in our lives, transforming the ambience of every meal. One thing led to another—consequences of the kind you can't and don't expect.

Someone heard that the church at the corner of King and Green next to the hospital might be a healing place, a forgiving place, a place with heart. Someone else experienced a longed-for flash of faith and hope. After all, such things had happened before, long ago: a dinner invitation, a crashed party, a jar of expensive perfume, and some kisses.[3] And for a few months many centuries later, it happened again, this time with roses. It

---

2. Nancy Vernon Kelly, "Something like Roses" in *See You Next Week: An Ecumenical Community Ministry in Downtown Kitchener* (Kitchener: Community Ministry), 47. Reprinted with permission.

3. Luke 7:36-50. *NRSV.*

happened among a diverse and unlikely gathering of people, each individual a consequence of God's love. One among them set in motion a unique way of saying thank you. And when she flew off into her new future, another took up her labor of love gathering and arranging roses, so the rest of us could behold ripples of glory that flowed from a florist's generosity.

The bounty of leftover roses ended after a time, as all such things do, yet the memory of their beauty and aroma remained—and the meals continued.

Each of us is a consequence of God's infinite love, and every day, from the dependable abundance of that love, we can draw on its power to respond with something like roses. Something like roses, to thank the One who prepares an eternal feast where we are all welcomed as honored guests. An expanding table where we all belong and know it.

The Food Voucher Binder

*"As any tracker of red admirals and monarchs will tell you,
all you can really do is feed the caterpillars."*

THE REV. DR. MARTHA TER KUILE[1]

1. Martha ter Kuile, Bloor Street United Church in Toronto, Ontario. Lenten email meditations, 2022. https://bloorstreetunited.org/.

I t was Wednesday again. The young man dashed in through the back laneway door, saying he needed a food voucher. He went straight to the Community Ministry office tucked into a tight corner of the church library. He knew where to go. The food voucher binder sat there, propped against the Community Minister's computer, waiting to be of service.[2]

The young man was sweet, and he was also angry. He had a long story. Most of us do. Here he was, in our faces again, pleading for help. This was before the time when people lined up in the church laneway early in the morning on Food Voucher Day. It was in the time before guidelines and quotas. The Community Minister filled out a food voucher for the market across the street and invited the man back for our community supper that evening.

It was a well-worn script. The young man danced out the front door onto King Street, whistling to himself. He wouldn't be at the supper. I *knew* he wouldn't be at the supper. I *knew* we wouldn't see him again until a few days before the end of the next month.

This time, the familiar script went awry. I was wrong—so utterly wrong that I've questioned what I know "from experience" ever since.

That afternoon, the same young man returned a couple of hours before the meal, dancing into the church kitchen with a big ham under his arm. "Guess what's for supper tonight?" he hollered. This man, with no money in the bank, and often no roof over his head, was smiling like an angel. He tied a gingham apron around his waist and kept right on dancing. He opened a cupboard, pulled down a roasting pan and shoved the big ham he'd bought with his food voucher into the oven to share with all the hungry folks who would gather later for supper. All I could do was shake my head in delighted disbelief—delighted to be so wrong about someone I thought I knew so well. Delighted to have the chance to cast someone in a new light. What if he is Christ's "humble dwelling?"[3]

2. Nancy Vernon Kelly, "Under the Influence" in *See You Next Week,* 54-56 Reprinted with permission.

3. Charles Wesley, "Lord, Divine, All Loves Excelling," *Evangelical Lutheran Worship.* (Minneapolis: Augsburg Fortress, 2006), No. 631.

Another fellow was already setting up tables and chairs as he always did, after spending an hour cleaning up cigarette butts outside the church's back door. Someone else was hanging around in bare feet, pleading with everyone who came in to play Crazy Eights with him. The artist was arranging roses in cheap milk glass vases and setting out candle stubs so we could dine by candlelight. The man who lived rough in nearby Mount Hope Cemetery and claimed to celebrate his birthday every day of the year, was in deep sleep, his head down on one of the tables. Near the stage, a friend from our partner church sat backwards in a Sunday School chair, playing "This Little Light of Mine" on his harmonica.

Around four o'clock, a woman came bearing hot dogs and salad. Another brought a casserole made with tofu for our vegetarian diners. A retired pastor came with an apple crisp he'd made, the fruit sliced as thin as parchment.

With a gentlemanly bow, an elderly man presented his offering of tinned beef stew. A teenaged boy wheeled in on his bicycle with buns from the Portuguese bakery. Meanwhile, several men knelt in the asphalt parking lot, shucking corn from a local farmer to go in a giant pot already boiling on the stove. In one of the ovens, pigtails and a twenty-pound turkey were roasting, both donated by an Old Order Mennonite farmer.

And in the other oven—the amazing food voucher ham.

We hadn't even said grace, yet here and there I could sense strong hints of the Presence "with a capital P."

It was soon hard to tell who was who. There must have been eighty of us in the church hall by then—or maybe a biblical five thousand. By 5:45 pm, many hands were on deck delivering food to the long serving table. We then formed a human circle that reached clear around the Parish Hall. And for one moment of deep-in-the-heart peacefulness, there was complete silence in the middle of the city.

"Anybody's birthday?" asked the woman who always let the children go first. "Yee ha!" hollered the woman in a cowboy hat, sitting in her usual place aboard her motorized scooter. "I'm eight years old today!"

Some of the men erupted in rude noises. Undeterred she yelled back, "Not my belly-button birthday, sillies! Eight years ago, I was raised from the dead!" A round of wild applause rose from the heart of our circle; someone dashed over to the piano and started banging out "Happy Birthday." The woman who'd been sober for eight years—and who knows how many others among us—basked in the glow of resurrection.

The woman who let the children go first then said grace. And the moment "Amen" was out of her mouth, one of the younger men from the corn-shucking group yelled "Go Broncos!" It was a little homegrown ritual of his, of ours, the cue for folks to start lining up on both sides of the serving table.

On Wednesday nights, there were some gentle rules about being sure to treat one another with respect and dignity, to honor each other and never to diminish anyone; but there were no rules to say that a young man couldn't buy a ham with his food voucher to feed a bunch of fellow hungry people. And there were no rules to say another young man couldn't yell "Go Broncos!" every single week, right after grace.

Sometimes you just see more than you can see with your physical eyes, and this was one of those times. That night, through the eyes of faith, I recognized Christ[4] wearing a red and white gingham apron and standing in the kitchen doorway, burdened by life yet radiant as he leaned into the room and helped feed the crowd. In that moment, he had a quiet, satisfied smile on his face. I wouldn't have been surprised if he'd lifted up his hands to bless us.

Soon I was recognizing Christ in the sweet, angry young man and also in the slicing of the ham, the faces of those who set the table, in all of us who lined up to fill our plates with ham, Portuguese buns, salad, corn-on-the-cob, hot dogs, and the rest of the given bounty. All this happened against the backdrop of coercive world powers that strive to lock us into boxes from which we're never meant to escape. Yet we do. It happened by the grace of God in a particular midtown church on a particular Wednesday night in history, at the intersection of King and Green Streets, one block

4. Luke 24:13-35. *NRSV.*

up from Central Fresh Market, in between the hospital and the high school, on the mainline bus route.

It was downright contrary and spectacular to see Christ at work that night, right here on earth, unlocking boxes we people think we'll never be able to escape from and making it a waste of time for us to try to size each other up.

The Back Door

*"It's about whether you feel yourself as a part
of this wild project about love."*

KATE BOWLER[1]

1. Krista Tippett, "On Being." Podcast episode "The Future of Hope." Interview with Kate Bowler and Wajahat Ali. (National Public Radio, September 16, 2021.) https://onbeing.org/programs/kate-bowler-and-wajahat-ali-the-future-of-hope. Retrieved November 21, 2022.

A s on most mornings, the security system was already disarmed by 6:30 AM. As usual, a soft glow and quiet murmuring radiated from the Parish Hall and kitchen of the old church next door to the high school. I loved those days when I arrived early enough to smell bacon the bacon sputtering on the griddle and share in the warmth and goodwill that inspired the Breakfast Club. That warmth and goodwill stuck with me all day.

Through the doors, I could see brightly-colored cloths and flowers on the tables. In the kitchen, teachers and volunteers from both partner churches and the wider community were buzzing around at various tasks. Some of the students had already finished breakfast. Besides the occasional treat of bacon and eggs, there was always oatmeal, bagels and cream cheese, strawberry jam, cold cereal and milk, muffins, waffles, toast, orange juice and yogurt. Sometimes even French toast.

When I arrived on that chilly March day, the early birds were already edging toward the church's back door, pulling on boots and coats, hoisting up their backpacks. I stood in the hall wishing them "Happy March Break" as they slipped out in time to get to their lockers before the start of classes.

As I stood by the back door, I don't remember hearing the bell yet. It must have been just about to ring when I noticed one lone student, looking down at the floor, dragging his feet and walking towards the door. Back in the days before the Breakfast Club started, was this the same boy who brought a handful of hard candies and a can of soda pop to school for lunch?

I smiled and wished the boy "Happy March Break," just as I had for all the others. This student, smaller than his peers, had tunneled into the hearts of both teachers and volunteers. He stopped, turned, looked me in the eye, and said "I don't want to go on vacation. I want to stay right here." I didn't have time to respond before the student disappeared through the back door. The memory lingered. I spent the rest of the day wondering what was going on for that student at home and in school and in the rest of his life.

A few months later, volunteers from the two host congregations and the high school held a special breakfast to celebrate the end of the school year. After the meal, some of the students and teachers went to the front of the Parish Hall with microphones to thank the volunteers. They gave out little pots of petunias to show their appreciation.

All at once, the same student who didn't want to go on March Break began to cry like a small child. I can't remember his exact words. Once again, he found his voice. This time he had the mic. He said something about moving away over summer vacation and that he didn't know if he would find a safe place at his new school. Life was one big question mark for him on a day when he must have been filled with what poet Madeleine L'Engle called "the panic clang of closing doors."[2]

I still remember how the student buried his head in a teacher's shoulder. And how the teachers, church volunteers and other students spontaneously drew close, formed a circle around him like a big protective hug, and wished him well through his tears and ours.[3] The breakfast became a time of blessing for a journey. We were all hugging each other—teachers, students, the 90-year-old woman who'd graduated from the same high school eons before, a couple of empty-nesters, a petite uniformed policewoman with four children of her own.

I liked it there too, in the church where the back door swung open every weekday morning for students to enter a safe and nourishing space for everybody. Including one small teenager who stood on a liminal threshold at a time when familiar doors were closing with a "panic clang" and the future was a fearful mystery.

2. Madeleine L'Engle, "Herman the Ezrahite" in *A Cry Like a Bell*. (Wheaton: Harold Shaw Publishers, 1987), 43.

3. 2 Corinthians 1:4, *NRSV.*

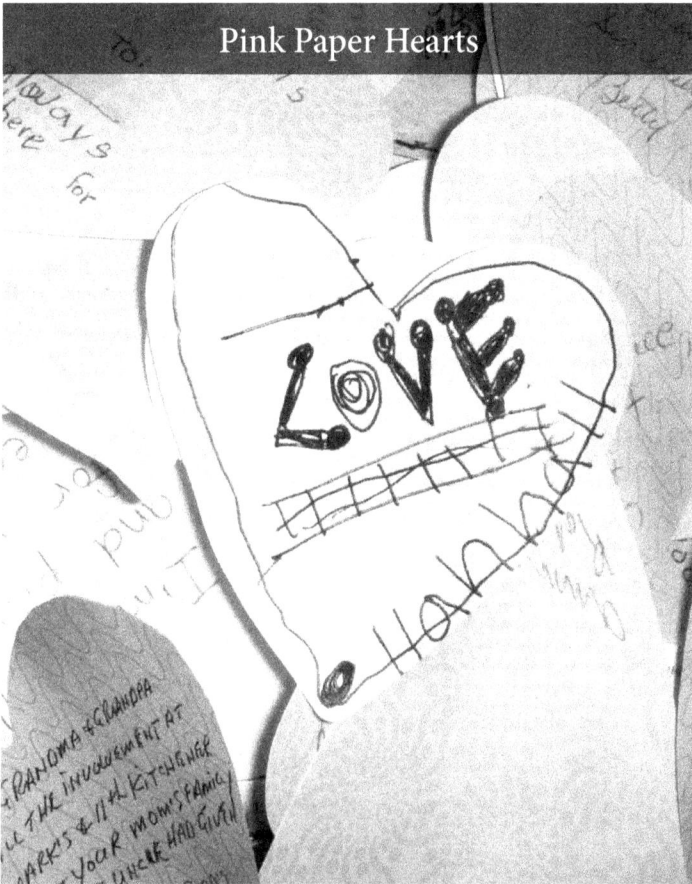

Pink Paper Hearts

"A new creation comes to life and grows."

JOHN B. GEYER[1]

---

1. John B. Geyer, "We Know That Christ is Raised" in *Evangelical Lutheran Worship*. (Minneapolis: Augsburg Fortress, 2006), No. 449. Music: Charles B. Stanford.

As often happens, along with the joy of a baptism, we were also filled with sadness, holding vigil for a young woman who was dying. At worship that morning, some of the woman's friends invited the congregation to write messages to her and her family on pink paper hearts. She had recently moved from the cancer center next to the church into a peaceful, light-filled rural hospice. We had been praying for her, for her husband, and for her young children. And now the time was drawing near for prayers to be answered—not in the way we had once hoped.

That morning, our typically lively pre-worship gathering time was hushed as people of all ages wrote notes, prayers, and drew pictures on little paper hearts. Even baptism visitors, who didn't know the woman or her family, wrote notes as the Music Director softly, like a whisper, played the baptismal hymn, "We Know that Christ is Raised and Dies No More."

Soon, all who were able stood to begin the service. When I looked out on our beloved congregation for the traditional pastoral Greeting, all I could see was wave upon wave of pink paper hearts. Everywhere. Many of us were wearing paper hearts over our flesh-and-blood hearts, as we sang:

> "We know that Christ is raised and dies no more.
>
> Embraced by death, he broke its fearful hold.
>
> And our despair he turned to blazing joy. Hallelujah!"[2]

After we baptized the baby—face down, so she could giggle and splash in the font's water of life—it was time for the Offering. By then, it was obvious that this entire service and all the people gathered together were the offering, filled with what Émile Durkheim[3] long ago recognized as "collective effervescence." We were coming together around one, simple loving thought.

I looked out into the pink-hearted sanctuary and my eyes misted. Ushers were coming forward with the bread and wine for Holy Communion, and the offering plates overflowed with pink

2. Geyer, 449.
3. Émile Durkheim, "Elementary forms of Religious Life," 1912.

paper hearts, fluttering like living butterflies—signs of love offered to God—to be delivered to the young woman at the hospice.

Later that afternoon, when I visited the young woman, she was sitting in bed, propped up with many pillows, watching a travel program on TV. It was as if she had already packed her bags, and she was focusing on the next great adventure. Someone from church had already visited[4] her, and the walls of the room were covered with pink paper hearts, filled with messages of love and support.

Once long ago, pink heart-shaped butterflies fluttered outside through the doors of a church and landed on the walls of the room where the young woman was dying. Those hearts have long since flown off to somewhere unseen except through the eyes of faith. Yet in that hospice, where someone else is now dying, out of infinite love for us, God is weaving together the wondrous threads of lives, deaths, and resurrections, turning despair into blazing joy[5] and sharing peace in every departure and arrival. A peace we cannot make for ourselves.

4. Galatians 6:2. *NRSV.*
5. Geyer, Ibid.

"O Christ, create new hearts in us that beat in time with yours,
that, joined by faith with your great heart,
become love's open doors."[1]

HERMAN STUEMPFLE

1. Herman G. Stuempfle, "O Christ, Your Heart Compassionate" in *Evangelical Lutheran Worship* (Minneapolis: 2006), *Worship),* No. 722.

On the surface of it, the purpose of our congregational meeting was to hold a simple yes-no vote. No more discussion. Just the vote. About a hundred people stayed in their pews after the service. They heard the motion read and cast their ballots on little slips of scratch paper. As far as I know, they had never before found it necessary to hold a congregational meeting before a wedding.

Swirling below the surface and up to the rafters was Jesus' commandment to love one another unconditionally, alongside the centuries-old oppression of queer, gay and non-binary people, so deeply entrenched in Judeo-Christian society. As the moments stretched out during the vote counting, I leaned against a back pew looking out over God's beloved, very quiet people.

In a front pew sat the couple preparing to be married. Scattered throughout the sanctuary were folk who hoped and had worked for a "yes" vote, side-by-side with those finding deep struggle in their decision. The lives and families of many throughout the congregation would be affected, one way or another, by the decision about to be revealed from those little slips of paper.

As I waited, a young man quietly rose from his pew and headed for the door near where I stood. We greeted one another. Then he paused. "I really wanted to be here to vote and hear the results . . . I want to stay, and I also have to get to work. I waited as long as I could."

At that moment, as on many other moments, how I wished we didn't need to have a vote. As the young man hurried out the door, my memory scrolled back to all that had happened, all that *had* to happen, to make this day and this decision even possible. The Adult Education sessions, the personal stories, the family stories, the private chats, the dinner table conversations, the newsletter articles, the sermons, the guest speakers, the national and synodical conventions, the town hall meetings. Several years earlier, same-sex marriage had become legal across Canada. Each of these small, collective steps played a role in the decision we were about to make.

At St. Mark's, the congregation included the faithful presence of two men who loved each other and wanted to spend the rest of their lives together. As the congregation awaited the ballot results, the couple sat in a front pew holding hands. I know they were holding hands because I felt the Spirit pull me gently forward to the front pew to sit beside them. I thought of my older sister, living in a same-sex partnership for more than fifty years; she had no church support at all, except when slipping quietly into Alcoholics Anonymous meetings in church basements.

My sister's story was tucked into my heart the day the two men first came looking for a new church home. Both had been baptized in other denominations and grew up in active church families. They showed up together at worship one Sunday morning and never left. Soon they were sharing their musical and leadership gifts in worship and staying for coffee hour. They had a disarming way of inviting young people to open up about their lives and also became beloved youth Sunday School class leaders. They affirmed their baptisms to become full members of the congregation. And they then they asked to be married in their church.

Time crawled, and after what seemed like a very long and intense wait, the scrutineers returned to the sanctuary and the chair announced a resounding "Yes"—not only to this wedding. To all future same-sex weddings. They would be celebrated like all other weddings, for two people in love with each other who wanted to be married in their home church in the presence of God, their families, and their friends. This vote was more than a "Yes" to marriage preparation talks and liturgy planning. Looking at the calendar and choosing a date. A procession. Vows. Rings. Prayers. A licence. Witnesses. Special music and other thoughtful touches. The vote was a resounding "Yes" to a new way of being the church of Christ.

In spring of the following year, I saw a worship guide cover unlike any I had seen before or ever imagined seeing in church: the silhouette of two grooms, thankfully far less remarkable now than it was then. Surrounded by loving support, these two grooms processed down the church's center aisle together and made their vows to one another.

St. Mark's was clearly their chosen congregation. What did come as a surprise was their decision to invite their entire faith community—children, youth, parents, everyone in the congregation, to celebrate their shared love and hear them promise to "live together in the covenant of marriage."[2]

These are the thoughts I offered in the brief homily just before the couple made their promises. As in every wedding, I spoke to the couple and invited everyone else to listen in.

After so much decision-making and planning and hoping and dreaming, today is the moment you've been waiting for. The rest of us have been waiting for this moment too!

It's worth mentioning where we are and where we aren't. We aren't at the Victoria Park Pavilion, which was Plan B, just in case. We are in your home church, where you longed to be married all along. So, the time has come, and the place is here, and you are you. Powerful signs of God's grace and companionship on your journey. We have much to thank God for as we celebrate the special gift you are to each other and the special gift you are to the rest of us, as you make your promises before God and this gathering of your family, your friends, and your church.

We met a number of times as you prepared for this day, and at one of our meetings you had a conversation with each other about what marriage means to you. I had the privilege of listening in on your conversation, and with your permission, I now repeat back to you some of what you said to each other. (It doesn't hurt for the rest of us to hear these words, too.)

Marriage is hope for the future. You hope the love and security you feel with each other will grow and deepen. In time, you hope to own a home and bring children into your family. You hope to be a blessing to your extended families. Beyond that, you hope to offer the world a picture of what relationships can be . . . two equal partners building a life together, both contributing. You hope to be a blessing to younger people, especially to younger LGBTQ+ people, and to all people who are working for social justice.

2. Service of Marriage, *Evangelical Lutheran Worship.* (Minneapolis: Augsburg Fortress, 2006), 287.

God is in the mix, too, the source of all love. You have been surprised by what you call "the unexpectedly good experience" you've had in the Christian community. This experience, you say, gives you stability. You affirm that your experience of God's love makes your bonding and your attachment with each other possible and gives you the resilience and strength you need to persevere through difficult times. You are very clear that the love you have for each other strengthens you to reach out to care for other people.

Not surprisingly, the two of you have given much careful thought to the words and the music for today. Fittingly, you chose a song about servanthood for all of us to sing together just before you make your promises to each other. Your choice of this song says a lot about the value you place on the teachings of Jesus and the kind of relationship you hope to build, an inspiration to us all.

As you prepare to make your vows to each other, the song you have chosen for all of us to sing along with you is "Will You Let Me Be Your Servant?"

And then the whole gathered community young and old rose up to offer each other earnest words of commitment and promise:

"Let me be as Christ to you."

"I will weep when you are weeping."

"When you laugh, I'll laugh with you."

"I will hold the Christ light for you."[3]

At the reception that evening, the chatter hushed after supper when the couple walked across the stage and sat down side-by-side on the piano bench at Victoria Park Pavilion. I don't remember the piece they played. It was as though we, their family, friends and church, had been listening to their heartfelt duet all along.

A faith community had voted to clear the way for this day. To receive the Gospel's lively pulse in our midst inhabiting something as mundane as parliamentary procedure. To break the bonds of oppression and set love free. It happened at the intersection of Gospel and Law.

3. Richard Gillard, "The Servant Song." *Evangelical Lutheran Worship* (Minneapolis: Augsburg Fortress, 2006), No. 659.

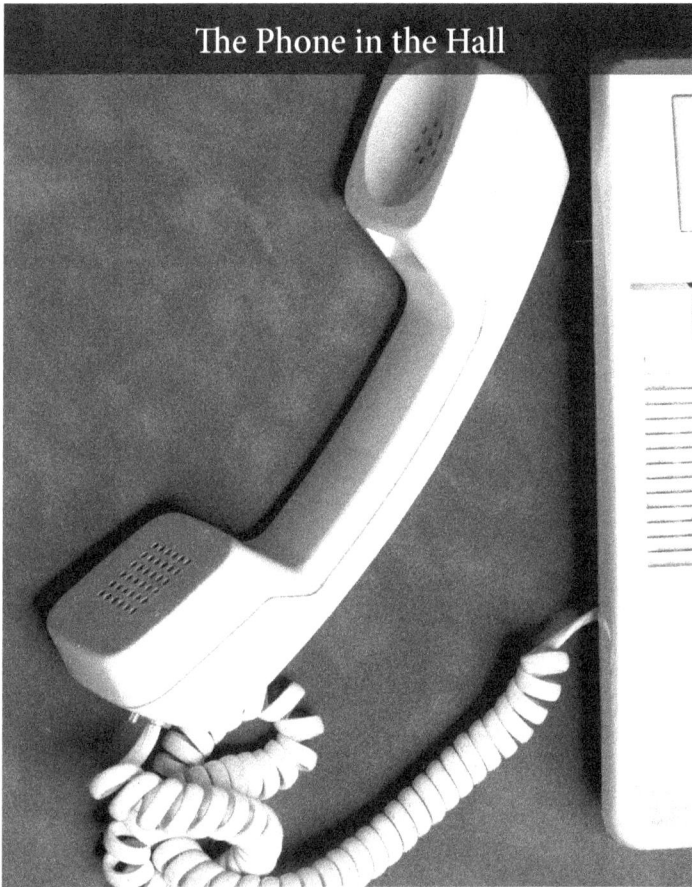

The Phone in the Hall

"There are some moments that become eternal."

ARIEL BURGER[1]

1. Ariel Berger, *Witness: Lessons from Elie Wiesel's Classroom.* (Toronto: HarperCollins, 2019), 246.

T he call came just after supper on a stormy Saturday evening. My home number was among those listed above the public phone in a first-floor alcove at church, to be used in case of emergency. As soon as I saw the originating number pop up, I sensed this was an S.O.S. call.

On the other end of the line, someone out-of-breath, anonymous in their urgency, told me that an old downspout had ruptured and rainwater was flooding the church basement where an Alcoholics Anonymous meeting was being held. They'd called the Fire Department, the custodian, and me. Floodwater was rising in the oldest part of the building where AA groups had long ago staked claim to an unused Sunday School room. There, Jesus hung on the wall presiding over 12 Step healing. That night, Jesus, ever-faithful, was also smiling down on the current calamity.

My husband and I sprang into action, grabbed our boots, jumped into the van and arrived at church to see a fire engine pulled up on the side street next to the building. Firefighters, our custodian, and members of the Property Committee were already downstairs, bailing water into the floor drain of the boiler room. After the firefighters left, the rest of us spent the evening bailing water together, laughing, and enjoying the camaraderie of team effort.

We never saw anyone from the AA group. By then, they were continuing on with their meeting. Yet they were the first ones to notice the flood, the first to realize it needed immediate attention. The first to call for help from anyone they could find. More than once I'd heard an AA member whisper how proud they were to be entrusted with a key to the church building and be responsible for unlocking and locking the doors.

The adults and high school students who came to 12 Step meetings considered the church to be their safe place. From time to time, church members would complain about the constant stream of people from the nearby Withdrawal Management (a.k.a. Detox) Center into "our" space. For many years, the building was a busy hive, the home to AA and other community support groups seven days a week. It wasn't surprising when friction arose from time to time over contested meeting spaces and for the provocative question, "Who belongs to this church?" to emerge. The flood was the prelude to another, infinitely more challenging question: "Who does the church belong to?" We posed that question and discussed it repeatedly and thoughtfully, yet we never arrived at an answer to satisfy everybody.

On the night of the flood, who did the space belong to? Clearly, the church was home to all of us. All of us owned the emergency. It was *our* emergency. The phone in a public place in the alcove on the main floor hall, the phone where the emergency numbers were posted, connected all of us together. That night, the phone was a phone for all of us. The point of connection.

And a specific, yet anonymous angel, a man in recovery who was sitting in a circle at an AA meeting in the basement under the picture of kind-hearted Jesus, willingly helped to overcome a specific emergency. Maybe he was the key holder in more ways than one!

Kind-hearted Jesus

"Everywhere around us is the terror and the wonder."

KATE BOWLER[1]

1. Krista Tippet, "On Being", on episode entitled "The Future of Hope," National Public Radio, September 16, 2021.https://onbeing.org/programs/kate-bowler-and-wajahat-ali-the-future-of-hope/. Retrieved November 23, 2022.

"*Dear Pastor,*

It has been ages since our paths crossed. You likely remember me as J_____. I once lived across the street at a high-rise apartment house. The church was so kind to bring me a Christmas Hamper way back. It must have been about sixteen years or so.

I felt prompted today by the Spirit to write you this letter to tell you just how instrumental the church has been in setting souls free from the bondage of addictions through AA to Al-Anon and all the many groups that meet at the church on a regular basis. I know of no other church in this area that has been so receptive to recovery 12 Step programs and has such a heart for the lost and broken.

When I got sober, I always felt that you folks had been praying for me all along, and I want to say thanks! I continued to attend AA at the church. Not only did I get very active in AA, I founded a group at another church. We outgrew that church two years ago, moved to yet another Lutheran church and have been going strong ever since.

It all began with your awesome Vacation Bible School. I would gladly drop my kids off for a couple hours so I could go to the liquor store in peace (or so I thought it was peace). The kids would come home and talk to me about Jesus. Apparently, the tremendous efforts of your staff paid off. Kids who wind up at places like your Bible School are there for a purpose only understood by God.

So, on behalf of all the AA groups and the Cool Friendship Group of Al-Anon, I want to say a heartfelt thanks. I have witnessed so many miracles at the church. The humble picture of Jesus has been a visual cue for many to step forward into the light. The very ones you would think would never give their whole lives to him—scoundrels and sick housewives—at the ends of their ropes. I am beyond gratitude to the church for the work Christ is doing. You have made an unspeakable difference in the lives of so many. You have no idea what respect our groups have for your church. That picture of Jesus hangs up above our heads. Always reminding us of who our "Higher Power" really is.

J."

Long ago J.'s words were shared with the Church Council and on Sunday morning with her encouragement and permission. Though she remains anonymous, her words are complete in themselves and tell her own story with heartfelt honesty, sincerity and grace. When life's terrors meet the liberating power of the Spirit, the wonder unleashed is as worthy of proclamation as the weekly reading of the gospel on Sunday mornings.

> "What is abiding in human life is the actual daily conversation
> that occurs in the very shadow of the monuments
> we raise to our abstract desires."

DAVID WHYTE[1]

---

1. David Whyte, *Consolations: The Solace, Nourishment and Underlying Meaning of Everyday Words* (Langley: Many Rivers, 2015, 212.

To: St. Mark's

From: MS

2 November

Apologize for being late with our contribution.

Where did October go?

We are working with 8 to 12 people each Monday.

Last week a new gentleman celebrated 30 days sober.

Next week, we will celebrate one year of sobriety for a young man who has "Returned" from _ _ _ _.

Your generosity is appreciated.

Endangered

*"In sacred manner may we walk
upon the fair and loving earth."*

Susan Palo Cherwien[1]

1. Susan Palo Cherwien, "In Sacred Manner." *All Creation Sings* (Minneapolis: Augsburg Fortress, 1990), No. 1071. The text of this hymn weaves together an indigenous American prayer and biblical imagery.

The retired factory worker was a lifelong member of the congregation. He sat in the back row of the choir loft just below the organ pipes. He was a bit bashful, usually not much of a talker. Once in a while, he'd lean up against the door frame of my study and get going on a subject he was interested in, like classical music or history.

This man had a magic touch with the church's old organ. He didn't play it; he was the go-to wizard when something went wrong. With precision, he fixed problems with the leathers and the pipes so the Property Committee didn't have to call in an expensive professional. In the workshop down in the church basement, with his own hands and skill, he fashioned new pipes to expand the organ's capacity.

He did the same with the boiler. It was as though the organ and boiler were among the man's most intimate friends, even his children. He knew their quirks. He tended them. He came to church on weekday mornings and sequestered himself down in the boiler room or the workshop, or up in the attic up above the chancel, tinkering with the machinery that made things work. He was a pro. No one on the Property Committee knew the boiler and organ like he did.

One quiet afternoon, I was standing by the front window of my upstairs study looking down on King Street in a sort of daze. The high school football players were on their way to practice in a field behind the TV station. People were waiting at bus stops on both sides of the main street. As usual, the city was bustling, yet the parking lot seemed to be resting for the moment. No cars pulling in or out.

From my vantage point, I didn't notice the small motionless gray lump on the asphalt. But someone else did, the organ and boiler man. Along he came, likely leaving the church after spending the morning tending one or the other. I watched this Good Samaritan[2] descend the stairs, notice a need, stop in his tracks beside his neighbor, and slowly kneel down. His presence drew my attention to the little gray lump, a particular dove with wings

2. Luke 10:25-37. NRSV.

meant to fly and a beak meant to forage and build nests and a mission to nurture new life. This dove was now either dead or wounded, lying on the asphalt.

For a long moment, it looked as though the man was whispering something to the dove, or praying, or maybe just sighing. He cupped his hands, lifted the bird, stood up, and gently cradled its limp body as he accompanied it to a patch of grass. There he laid the dove to rest in peace.

For a long, silent moment, for the love of Creation, a vision of goodness and mercy appeared in the front parking lot of a midtown church.

Saint Francis and the Farting Dog

"When we see each other through the eyes of wonder, all barriers,
all differences disappear. We are alive. We have joined."

RICHARD WAGAMESE[1]

1. Richard Wagamese, *Embers: One Ojibway's Meditations* (Madeira Park:
Douglas McIntyre, 2016), 162.

T hough the October morning was sunny and warm outside, the inside of the church felt clammy and cold. When I heard music coming from the sanctuary, at first, I thought it was the Music Director practicing her clarinet. But no. I stopped and listened again. It wasn't the Music Director practicing her clarinet. The sound I heard was both robust and mellow. Almost as if there were many musicians making music together.

I tiptoed into the transept, and peeked around the corner to see a long-retired member of the local symphony sitting on a little Sunday School chair in front of the chancel. He wasn't alone. His dog, infamous and not overly popular at church for farting during Worship and Music Committee meetings, was curled up in front of the chancel tethered to the communion rail. Breathing deeply beside his master.

On the day commemorating Saint Francis of Assisi, patron saint of animals and stowaways (as we'd learned in devotions at the Worship and Music Committee earlier that morning), this brilliant old musician was playing "Make Me a Channel of Your Peace" on his euphonium. It seemed as though he was serenading his beloved bulldog, the dog he called "My son." The sound of the euphonium filled the darkened sanctuary with a burst of warm, soothing resonance and heavenly light. Though the man never knew I was listening, his music filled me too, with holy awe.

God was inside the darkness. God was inside the old man's musical breath. And God was even inside the digestive system of that problematic dog. God was surely in the music itself and in the making of the music. And God was in the listening. The whole equaled much more than the sum of its parts.

And all the bits and pieces came together, as bits and pieces sometimes do, in the expansive prayer attributed to Saint Francis of Assisi:

> *Lord, make me an instrument of your peace:*
> *where there is hatred, let me sow love;*
> *where there is injury, pardon;*
> *where there is doubt, faith;*

where there is despair, hope;
where there is darkness, light;
where there is sadness, joy.

O divine Master, grant that I may not so much seek
to be consoled as to console,
to be understood as to understand,
to be loved as to love.
For it is in giving that we receive,
it is in pardoning that we are pardoned,
and it is in dying that we are born to eternal life.
Amen."[2]

---

2. Translation of *Belle prière à faire pendant la Messe* first published in *La Clochette*, n° 12, Dec. 1912. The original work and this translation are in the Public Domain.

The Bowl of Mints

St. Mark's Lutheran Church

growing in faith, caring, and community

"Things are happening in order to take you somewhere."

FREDERICK BUECHNER[1]

1. Frederick Buechner, *The Remarkable Ordinary* (Grand Rapids: Zondervan, 2017), 59.

The Office Manager, a devoted, lifelong member of the church, kept a little bowl of Scotch mints on the ledge above her desk. When passing through the office, many people would grab a mint or two and enjoy a little visit with her. Including our mail carrier. Instead of depositing the stack of envelopes and flyers in the mail box outside the church, this particular mail carrier made his way to the office to deliver them personally.

On these everyday occasions, the mail carrier, like so many others, popped a mint or two in his mouth and chatted with whoever else happened to be around that morning. He was one of many neighborhood "regulars" who dropped by the church. A delightful, outgoing neighbor. This story is beginning to sound like an episode of Mister Rogers' Neighborhood!

One day the Music Director happened to be in the church office just when the mail carrier was passing through, and the two of them launched into the first of many conversations about life in general, and particularly about music. It turned out that the mail carrier loved to play flute and guitar, and was very good at both.

"Sometime," the Music Director ventured, "How would you like to play at one of our services?"

The mail carrier said yes, and so began an engaging decades' long conversation between the congregation and the mail carrier. Next thing, he appeared at the Christmas Eve candlelight service to accompany "Silent Night" on his guitar, the way it was originally written to be sung like a lullaby.

Then he began showing up on Sunday mornings to play with the worship band and hang out with the other band musicians. Now and then he played his flute to accompany the liturgy, Senior Choir anthems, or soloists.

When the Office Manager with the mint dish retired, the congregation made sure the mail carrier was invited to attend her potluck lunch celebration. At just the right moment, he arrived at the party with his mail bag, zoomed into the Parish Hall through the back door, and landed right beside the Office Manager. *Voila!* He shook out a load of grateful, affectionate retirement cards and gifts from his stuffed mailbag. Special Delivery!

In a time when all over the world, and close by, many signs of relatedness and belonging were breaking down, many little bridges, built in kindness, led from one beautiful sign of kinship to another.

Mail.

Mints.

Music.

More.

Amen.[2]

2. Romans 12:5. *NRSV.*

The Crying Pew

"Wonder is the inexhaustible foundation...,
the ground of our creative expectation of the new day."

JÜRGEN MOLTMANN[1]

---

1. Jürgen Moltmann, *God for a Secular Society: The Public Relevance of Theology* (London: SCM Canterbury, 1999), 146.

The beloved seminary New Testament professor sat in the same pew every Sunday morning, right behind my husband, our daughters, and our grandchildren. He often had his Greek New Testament open in his lap so he could read along and ponder the pulse of the Gospel in its original language.

Everybody knew this man as a wise scholar, a wholly devoted disciple of Jesus. He was well known for standing up in meetings and conventions to speak sharp and courageous truths to power about a wide range of social issues, including poverty, racism, climate change, same-sex marriage and the ordination of LGBTQ+ people. He also emanated tender loving kindness whenever he perceived someone to be vulnerable and overlooked. Through the lens of grace, he could see someone at risk, and also their God-given dignity and potential.

During the postlude on Sunday mornings, he would often quietly make his way to the church entrance facing King Street, our city's main thoroughfare. He wasn't making a quick getaway. He was filled with another purpose. While he chose to sit in at the end of one of the front pews during worship, with his special radar, he also knew what was going on in the very back pew.

This brilliant historian lived very much in the present moment; he knew when someone slipped into church late and sat alone in the back. He felt that tingle, that prompting in his soul, the internal call to make a connection. And he did.

Over the years, the professor came to call that place at the very back "The Crying Pew." Time and time again someone came in late, sat down at a distance from everyone else, and began (or continued) to weep. The professor knew that this spot was exactly where he was called to be.

And he went.

He would sit down in the last pew and pay gentle attention. Sometimes he offered a few soft and simple words of consolation like "There, there," but I doubt he pried. And from the improbable space of "The Crying Pew" came story after story of celebration and new life. Stories for others to tell about how God-with-us weeps with us in our need and calls us to weep with one another, until the day we are astonished that at last all our tears are wiped away.[2]

---

2. Revelation 7:17, Revelation 21:4. NRSV.

All Saints' Day

All Saints' Day is a time to light candles and say prayers and name the names of those dear to us who have died in the previous year. It's a time to toll bells and remember and give thanks for all departed lives. All Saints' Day is also a day set aside to remember and give thanks that all of us, old and young, who bear the cross of Christ are saints. We belong to one Body of Christ created to be whole, though often fractured.

This story is about the time a restless, elderly prophet near the end of his life led an unexpected procession of much younger saints (two to be exact!) through the nave of the church.

The Procession

"These stones that have echoed their praises are holy,
and dear is the ground where their feet have once trod."

WILLIAM HENRY DRAPER[1]

1. William Henry Draper, "In Our Day of Thanksgiving." *Evangelical Lutheran Worship* (Minneapolis: Augsburg Fortress, 2006), No. 229.

One day, the beloved old gentleman came to church on a weekday afternoon on the arm of his eldest daughter. He'd been away for a long time. A few years earlier he used to drop by the church on summer weekday mornings to deliver his offering envelope . . . and a fried Giant Puffball mushroom. He'd foraged the mushroom at his cottage outside of town on the edge of a forest. He lovingly dredged the mushroom slices in milk, flour and whipped eggs, then sautéed the fat slices in sizzling butter. Then, he delivered this amazing, scrumptious treat—a big, spongy hunk of fungus that looked like a brain—just for the church staff.

While the church staff took a break and indulged, the man would lean against the office door frame smiling, chuckling, shooting the breeze. He remembered his wife. He remembered the house nearby where he grew up. He remembered the house where he and his wife raised their nine children. He remembered his younger brother, a pastor in another town.

The day the old man came back to church on his daughter's arm, he was off the usual map. He was no longer driving to his cottage, or delivering Giant Puffballs to his friends, or telling stories about the old days. By then, he was mostly far away in the miasma of dementia, needing more and more care. The question hanging in the air that day was: Would he still recognize his church and make a connection?

The first clue that he was still able to make the church connection: he'd shaved!

His daughter drove him to church partly to get him out of his apartment for some fresh air and a change of scenery. And partly to receive communion . . . because she knew communion was important to him. And partly because she wanted to see if the sanctuary she'd grown up in with its rich, carved wood and beams of rainbow-colored light filtering through stained-glass windows, might trigger a little spark of recognition through her father's mental fog. Bringing him to church was her labor of love. Shaving was his.

Well, the feel of the brittle little wafer in the old man's mouth, and the sweet fragrance of the wine he gulped from the silver chalice did seem to wiggle loose a memory or two. From deep in his mind, he still knew exactly how and when to respond. He still remembered how to bow his head, fold his hands for prayers, and weave his fingers into a little manger to receive the Meal.[2]

I don't know where his next move came from. It certainly wasn't anything his daughter and I said or did. And I doubt he'd ever said or done anything like it before either. As soon as we said the final "Amen," he shot out of the pew as if a Roman candle had gone off underneath him, and began marching up and down the sanctuary aisles shouting, "Amen. Amen. Forever and ever! Amen! Amen!"[3]

What could his daughter and his pastor do but the obvious? Right there, on a weekday afternoon in the old midtown church, we fell into step behind this unlikely witness. Up and down the aisles we marched in procession. Forever and ever! Amen! Side, center, front aisles. And again, side, center, front aisles, keeping up with the old man's swift, driving beat. With one voice, all three of us boisterously shouted "Amen! Amen! Forever and ever! Amen! Amen!"

Were we vigorously, rowdily hopeful? Declaring our primary allegiance like Saint Paul did to the first smitten Christians not long after Christ was raised from the dead? "To God be the glory forever and ever! Amen! Amen!"

Were we affirming our faith in God, as we do at the end of the Lord's Prayer? "For yours is the kingdom, the power and the glory. Forever and ever! Amen! Amen!?

Or were we boldly pulling onto the most gracious and spacious highway, still burdened and yet merging into a glorious vision, singing in unison with Handel's iconic Hallelujah Chorus? "And He shall reign forever and ever. Amen! Amen!"

Our collective response was likely a tangled up, heartfelt mix of all the above. Embedded in memories of the past and in the

---

2. Attributed to Martin Luther. As we sometimes teach in Confirmation, our outstretched hands at communion make a little manger for the Body of Christ.

3. John 8:32, *NRSV.*

concerns and courage of the present. Rising up from somewhere deep within our souls in lamentation and in hope. Hollered out in confession and in prophecy.

With the old man in the lead, we lifted our voices to God with tears and smiles as the complex layers of our response were gathered up into one movingly glorious benediction. "Forever and ever. Amen! Amen!"

Reign of Christ

I find the final Sunday of the Church Year, Reign of Christ, to be problematic because it tempts us to turn our attention exclusively to a triumphant and glorious Christ in some far-off end-time. The day used to be called Christ the King, which was even more problematic. Christ a king? But what sort of king? A fabulously wealthy ruler dressed in finery who inherits power and demands obedience from everyone below him on the social and economic ladder?

How much less challenging and more acceptable, and how much less disruptive and more well-mannered it would be to skip the real story entirely, especially the cross. To fast-forward beyond the human pain and suffering and miss the gifts available to us at the intersection of death and resurrection.

Beginning to encounter the heart of the Reign of Christ does not allow us to skip the dreadfulness of the cross. Nor to forget that before Jesus suffers and dies, he prepares his disciples to follow him by telling them telling stories. During his brief ministry, he invites us to lean in to the mysterious potential that's deep-down in God's economy (or God's household). He speaks in the present tense. It's like a tiny mustard seed, he says, teeming with life.[1] It belongs to little children who are infinitely valuable in their vulnerability and hold more wisdom than their elders might

1. Matthew 13:31-32. *NRSV.*

think.[2] It's like a banquet with unlikely guests.[3] It's like the yeast that bubbles up enthusiastically in warm water, ready to leaven the whole nutritious loaf.[4] God's economy, God's household is *now!*

2. Matthew 18:3. *NRSV.*
3. Luke 14:15-24. *NRSV.*
4. Matthew 13:33. *NRSV.*

Tale of Two Crowns

"Can you imagine a king born in a barn?
Wow! I sure can't!"

WILLIAM NHANALA, AGE 8[1]

1. From a child's telling of the Christmas story as he wrote it long ago on a window pane in colorful glass markers.

At a mid-week evening service just before Reign of Christ Sunday, two crowns were placed on the small table at the front of the small transept where we gathered for worship. One crown was golden with plastic jewels, salvaged from an old Halloween costume; the other was the crown of real thorns we hung over a rough-hewn cross on Good Friday when we remembered how Jesus died.[2]

There these two crowns sat, poles apart and side-by-side, while we listened to Jesus say to us, "My kingdom is not from this world."[3] We sat side by side, too: the woman who asked lots of questions, a few others who often spoke up thoughtfully and a gentleman named Arthur who never said a word.

At each mid-week service after someone read the Gospel for the following Sunday, we talked about what we had heard. We led off our reflection that evening with a question. What did Jesus mean when he said, "My kingdom is not from this world"?

Right away the woman who was endlessly curious fired a question back. Actually, two questions in one. "Is this just somebody trying to brainwash us or is it true?"

Many of us ask the same thing, I said. Did somebody make up this Jesus story or is it for real? Is it a lie or something we can trust, something we can bank our lives on? I liked the woman's question a lot and told her so.

I must whisper something to you now because you just have to try to see it. Something impulsive and sort of madcap had happened. By the time the woman asked her question, the golden crown was no longer up front. It was now perched atop Arthur's head. In other words, the golden crown had moved. Or been moved! Sometimes, people kidded around with Arthur, calling him "How Great Thou Art" and so it was fitting, in a way, to see the golden crown perched on his head. There he was, a good sport enjoying his moment in the spotlight, as many of us would. Yet among us and within us we harbored so many stories about how hurtful it is to be made fun of, as Jesus was made fun of when the

2. Nancy Vernon Kelly, "Tale of Two Crowns" previously published in *See You Next Week*, 97-98. Reprinted with permission.

3. John 18:36, *NRSV.*

crowd mocked him on the cross. We wouldn't have dared to clown around with the crown of piercing thorns which by then stood alone atop the little table front and center in the transept.

Anyway, the golden crown was still on top of How Great Thou Art's head, albeit askew, and it was quite a sight. The same woman who spoke up with such commendable doubt just moments earlier, spoke up for a second time. She was taking the story so seriously. "The golden crown," she announced, "is synthetic, and the crown of thorns is natural."

And the skeptical woman was telling the truth. Even a crown of real gold isn't worth much in the long run, and a crown of thorns hurts like hell when it digs into your scalp.

So, this is Christ the King, the one whom we worship. Firstborn of Mary and firstborn of the dead. The suffering servant and the ruler of the kings of the earth. He welcomes us to come to him like little children and says the first shall be last and the last shall be first. He calls to us from the cross that exposes the world's lies like that gaudy Halloween crown on How Great Thou Art's head. And he calls to us from the empty tomb to reveal to us the wonder of all that's spacious and loving and hopeful and true.

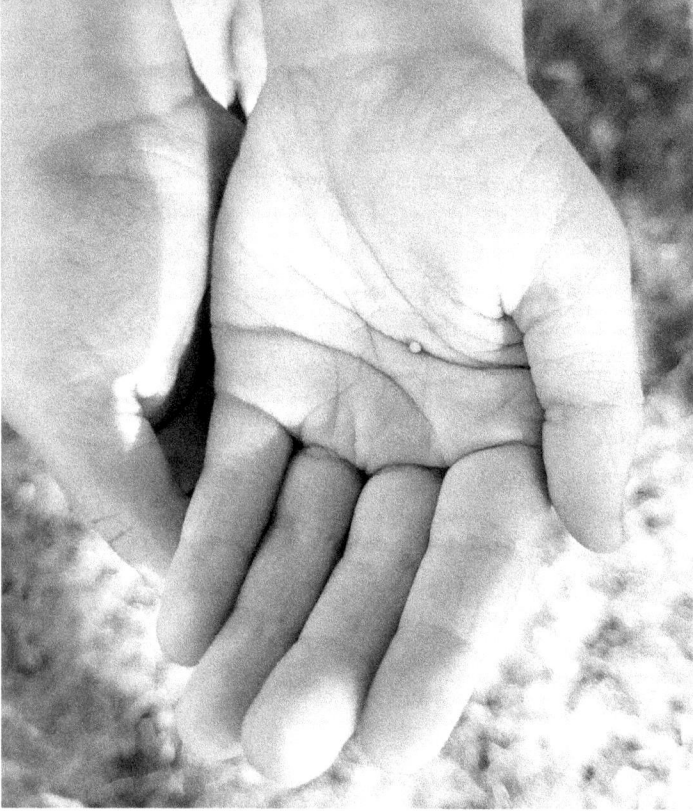

Small and Extravagant

"The Kingdom of Heaven is like a mustard seed."

JESUS[1]

1. Matthew 13:31-32. *NRSV.*

T his final story (until more of yours come alive in the telling!) is another story about the host—the one who brewed and poured the coffee and who personally invited two strangers (and probably countless others) to stay for supper.[2]

Every year, when an appeal went out for funds to send kids to church summer camp, the little boy who wanted to go to camp, who became the man who became the host, remembered growing up in a large family. Back then, he and his twin sister scoured parking lots and construction sites to collect enough deposits from used pop bottles to pay for half of their camp fees. Anonymous church friends gave the balance to pay for him and his siblings to attend camp.

Years later, when the boy had grown to adulthood, after work he liked to hang out at a local coffee shop with his buddies. Whenever the cashier handed back his coffee change, he did something very simple. He took the coins home and saved them in margarine containers. When the annual summer camp appeal came around, he brought his stash of loose change to church along with his regular offering envelope.

What joy was sparked when the ushers came up the middle aisle during the Offertory to present a heavy bag of coins along with the usual envelopes and cash on the plates! Probably many besides me were tickled to behold this unwieldy generosity. Our delight spilled over in a spirit of celebration. The counters had to stay longer than usual after worship to count and roll all those pennies, nickels, dimes, quarters, loonies and toonies. And some over the years just might have, understandably, let out a few exaggerated groans. But I don't remember any real complaining.

Over time, in a dazzling exchange, the child who had once been the guest of others became the host. The coins he saved always totaled enough to send at least one child to camp.

All of us, like the host, were in the past and are now in the present, characters living in the middle of a story. While the church is always *telling* a story with moral and mortal implications, faith

2. This story is told with the permission of "The Host." Written permission on file.

147

communities everywhere are also always *doing* a story with both moral and mortal consequences. Each guest (and who *isn't* a guest?) has the potential to become a host. And more than that, in God's hopeful economy, each guest is *worthy* of becoming a host.

Christ reigns like this. In small, extravagant ways. Feeding five thousand people with five loaves and two fish, turning the other cheek, chatting with a woman at a well, washing dirty feet, visiting the sick, riding on a donkey, sharing meals.

Postlude

S tories have a way of mapping both God's movements and ours. Taken all together these little stories are more than an ode to the lively pulse of the Gospel in a particular place. These stories bear witness to the good news that God is still coming to us beyond our most thoughtful planning and strategizing to lead us somewhere good and merciful. Though often hidden, the Spirit of God is always pulsing in our midst, inviting our attention and giving us clues about future directions.

I'm not sure where the tongues of fire are these days or the burning bushes. What I trust more than ever is this: God's goodness and mercy are still lub-dubbing, longing to restore all Creation into a one whole, communal, inclusive, generous, safe, peaceful, hopeful and thankful way of life for everybody. No one is ever invalidated in this way of life, and everyone is a bearer of gifts for the common good that come from the hand of God's gracious abundance.

The church needs everybody's gifts, including gifts we might never ask for that are now hiding in places we would never suspect, within those whom we might easily overlook or would rather turn away from. Take heart! These gifts are lavishly available all around us. And within us, too.

So where do you place yourself and your congregation in the movements of this life where it's so easy to dwell on the rough spots, fear, loneliness, greed, decline, destruction, danger, injustice and despair? The rough spots really are rough! And yet, as Gregg Gonsalves asks, "What would it mean to move into a future in which a common fate mattered as much as our own?" A common fate where "no one is disposable"?[1] How are you already going beyond your old map?

In unsettled times, wherever and whenever we sense the pulse of God's goodness and mercy (and even when we think we *might* sense that Presence with a capital "P"), how can we keep paying attention and tell each other what we are sensing? How can we also leave space open for each other to acknowledge our earnest hopes and fears? Especially when life leaves us overwhelmed, befuddled, gob-smacked, thrown for a loop, knocked out of kilter, when we realize we're veering off the known map into uncharted waters, what helps us look for opportunities to experiment with doing something more than just being anxious and fearful?

At these unsettled times of change, which are real and often seem to be ganging up on us, the pulse of goodness and mercy is still afoot in stations of wonder along the way to point us in the direction of a more hopeful, transformed life. A life where "from the bondage of sorrow, all the captives dream dreams."[2] A life where everybody matters. A life where *you* matter.

Every day, on the cusp of the future, what stories do you see unfolding at the ragged edges of damage, grief and the hope for healing? What seeds beyond the seeds you yourself planted are sprouting up in the open cracks between fear and the possibility of trust? Where is the heart within the heartbreak? Where is the dignity buried within many layers of indignity? Who is just barely catching their first breath of new life within the end of the old? Or could be?

And, how are you going to tell the story? Because—*here* be wonders, in the intersection of the treasures and tensions God is

1. Gregg Gonsalves, "The Moral Danger of Declaring the Pandemic Over Too Soon," *New York Times*, February 17, 2022. https://www.nytimes.com/2022/02/17/opinion/aids-pandemic-covid.html. Retrieved May 15, 2022. Gonsalves is a long-time AIDS activist and professor of Epidemiology at Yale University.

2. James K. Manley, "Spirit, Spirit of Gentleness." *Evangelical Lutheran Worship.* (Minneapolis: Augsburg Fortress, 2006), No. 396.

laying bare right now in uncharted waters. *Here,* the pulse of God's goodness and mercy still abides. This pulse has the power and the yearning to raise us up from our fears and give us new life we haven't yet imagined. Open your hand. This is for you.

Dear is the Ground[1]

Long ago, many were forced from this beloved land.
Sometimes, in the silence, I hear their voices.
Now others are coming to put down roots.
In wiggly time, I hear their voices, too.
Even the dead and the hungry are speaking.
Look! Some are shucking corn right over there.
A big pot of water is already boiling on the stove.
Folks are sitting at the long table, waiting for the meal to begin.
And over there is the woman with the satin flower on her cane.
The man who sweeps up the cigarette butts is in the laneway
with his broom
while a woman hums as she sets out chocolates at each place.
In the kitchen, the matriarchs are buttering slices of bread
to the edges.
A grandmother is serving *pflaumenkuchen*[2]
fromthe Old Country.
Two sisters fly through the door to deliver loaves
of Guyanese sweet bread,
And look!
Here comes someone else.
Someone we don't recognize.
Who is this stranger, sitting down, hoping to share the meal?
Maybe they'll stay awhile.
And put down roots.
Who will be *we* then?

---

1. The title of this poem comes from the All Saints' Day hymn: "In Our Day of Thanksgiving", text by William Henry Draper. *Evangelical Lutheran Worship* (Minneapolis: Augsburg Fortress, 2006), No 429.

2. Plum cake.

Bibliography

Brooks, Phillips: Text. Lewis H. Redner, Music. "O Little Town of Bethlehem."
Public Domain. *Evangelical Lutheran Worship*. Minneapolis: Augsburg
Fortress, 2006. No. 279.

Brown, Ariana. "For everyone who tried on the slipper before Cinderella." ©
2022 by Ariana Brown. Originally published in Poem-a-Day on October
14, 2022, by the Academy of American Poets.

Browning, Robert. "Abt Vogler." 1864, Public Domain.

Budde, Mariann Edgar. Sermon, Washington National Cathedral, August 29,
2021.

Buechner, Frederick. Online quote of the day. https://www.frederickbuechner.
com/quote-of-the-day/2018/4/3/eternity. Retrieved April 2, 2022.

Burger, Ariel. *Witness Lesson from Elie Wiesel's Classroom*. Boston: First Mariner
Books edition, Houghton Mifflin Harcourt, 2019.

Cherwien, Susan Palo. "In Sacred Manner," text of No. 1071 in *All Creation
Sings*. Minneapolis: Augsburg Fortress, 2020.

Colvin, Tom. "Jesu, Jesu, Fill Us with Your Love." *Evangelical Lutheran Worship*.
Minneapolis: Augsburg Fortress, 2006.

Coman, Sherry. *Lutherans Connect*. Lenten devotions, 2022. https://www.
blogger.com/profile/00877799114320166542.

Communauté de Taizé. 1991. "Within Our Darkest Night." *Les Presses de Taizé,*
GIA Publications Inc., agent.

Draper, W.H. "Our Day of Thanksgiving." *Evangelical Lutheran Worship*.
Minneapolis: Augsburg Fortress, 2006.

Dufner, Delores. "O Christ What Can It Mean for Us?" *Evangelical Lutheran
Worship,* Minneapolis: Augsburg Fortress, 2006.

Durkheim, Émile. "The Elementary forms of the Religious Life," 1912. https://
www.gutenberg.org/files/41360/41360-h/41360-h.htm. Retrieved August
29, 2023.

Eliot, T.S. "Dry Salvages." *Four Quartets*. Boston: Mariner Books, 1943. Copyright renewed by Esme Valerie Eliot, 1971.

Fredrickson, Dale. "on wounds & wonder," Steubenpress.com, © Dale Carl Fredrickson, 2017.

Geyer, John B. "We Know That Christ is Raised." Music: Charles B. Sanford. *Evangelical Lutheran Worship*. Minneapolis: Augsburg Fortress, 2006.

Gillard, Richard. "The Servant" Song. *Evangelical Lutheran Worship*. Minneapolis: Augsburg Fortress, 2006.

Gonsalves, Gregg. "The Moral Danger of Declaring the Pandemic Over Too Soon." *New York Times*, February 17, 2022. https://www.nytimes.com/2022/02/17/opinion/aids-pandemic-covid.html. Retrieved May 15, 2022.

Guite, Malcolm. "A Sonnet Based on the Transfiguration." *Sounding the Seasons*. London: Canterbury. https://malcolmguite.wordpress.com/2022/08/06/a-sonnet-on-the-transfiguration-3. Retrieved August 28, 2022.

Haugen, Marty. "Here Begins the Good News." *The Song of Mark*. Chicago: GIA Publications, 1996.

Kamieńska, Anna. "Small Things." *Astonishments: Selected Poems of Anna Kamieńska*. Brewster: Paraclete. Grazyna Drabik and David Curzon, trans. 2007.

Richard Kearney. *On Stories: Thinking in Action*. London: Routledge & Francis Group, 2002.

L'Engle, Madeleine. "Herman the Ezragite." *A Cry Like a Bell*. Wheaton: Harold Shaw Publishers, 1987.

Makeever, Ray. *Death Be Never Last*. Minneapolis: Augsburg Fortress, 2020.

Malebranche, Nicolas. "The Search after Truth." Public Domain.

Manley, James K. "Spirit, Spirit of Gentleness." *Evangelical Lutheran Worship*. Minneapolis: Augsburg Fortress, 2006.

Mathai, Philip. Sermon, Mount Zion Lutheran Church, Waterloo ON, Canada. April 3, 2022.

Meyer, Robinson. "No Old Maps Actually Say 'Here Be Dragons': But an ancient globe does." *The Atlantic* (online edition), December 12, 2013. https://www.theatlantic.com/technology/archive/2013/12/no-old-maps-actually-say-here-be-dragons/282267/. Retrieved August 26, 2022.

Mohr, Joseph. "Silent Night." *Evangelical Lutheran Worship*. Minneapolis: Augsburg Fortress, 2006. Original German text and music: Franz Gruber. Public Domain.

Moltmann, Jürgen. "God for a Secular Society: The Public Relevance of Theology." London: SCM Canterbury, 1999.

National Geographic Society. "Here Be Dragons," an online educational resource on cartography at https://education.nationalgeographic.org/resource/here-be-dragons. Retrieved August 2, 2022.

Ó Tuama, Pádraig. "Imagining Peace," TEDx talk, October 18, 2016. https://www.youtube.com/watch?v=lJfBYz6tab8. Retrieved August 16, 2022.

Pawlikawski, John. "Interpreting the Passion Narratives without Blaming 'the Jews.'" Boston College, Christian Scholars Group, a collaboration of the

Council of Centers on Jewish-Christian Relations. https://youtu.be/-woUhw_xPbk. Retrieved June 2, 2022.

Pierpoint, Folliott S. "For the Beauty of the Earth." Public Domain. Text of No. 879 in *Evangelical Lutheran Worship*, Minneapolis: Augsburg Fortress, 2006.

Rohr, Richard. Daily online meditation, *Being Present to the Presence of God*. Center for Action and Contemplation, November 12, 2021. https://cac.org/daily-meditations/being-present-to-the-presence-of-god-2021-11-12/. Retrieved July 18, 2022.

Shaw, Marilyn; Remus, Harold; Kelly, Nancy Vernon, Eds. *See You Next Week: An Ecumenical Ministry in an Ontario Downtown*. Kitchener: Community Ministry, 2007.

Solnit, Rebecca. *Hope in the Dark: Untold Histories, Wild Possibilities*. New York: Nation Books, 2004.

_____. *Orwell's Roses*. New York: Viking, 2021.

Stuempfle, Herman G. "O Christ, Your Heart Compassionate." *Evangelical Lutheran Worship*. Minneapolis: Augsburg Fortress, 2006.

ter Kuile, Martha. Lenten email meditations, 2022. Bloor Street United Church, Toronto, Ontario.

Tippett, Krista. "Letter to Friends of 'On Being.'" National Public Radio website, March 24, 2022. https://onbeing.org/blog/a-letter-from-krista-to-our-listeners/.

Wagamese, Richard. *Embers: One Ojibway's Meditations*. Madeira Park: Douglas McIntyre, 2016.

Wesley, Charles, "Love Divine, All Loves Excelling," *Evangelical Lutheran Worship*. (Minneapolis: Augsburg Fortress, 2006), No. 631.

Westermeyer, Paul. *Hymnal Companion to Evangelical Lutheran Worship*. Minneapolis: Augsburg Fortress, 2010.

Whyte, David. *Consolations: The Solace, Nourishment and Underlying Meaning of Everyday Words*. Langley: Many Rivers, 2015.

Wismayer, Henry. "Why Space Tourists Won't Find the Awe they Seek," *New York Times Magazine*, November 27, 2021.

Here Be Wonders:
The Gospel's Pulse

St. Mark's Place, 43 units
of supportive housing
sponsored by InDwell.

https://indwell.ca/st-marks-place
Retrieved August 6, 2023

All book royalties donated
to St. Mark's Place.

Printed in the USA
CPSIA information can be obtained
at www.ICGtesting.com
JSHW010905300624
65553JS00004B/12

9 798385 212590